hartz IV moebel .com

Build More, Buy Less

Konstruieren statt konsumieren

Edited by / Herausgegeben von
Van Bo Le-Mentzel
Texts by / Texte von **Birgit S. Bauer, Kristin
Hensel, Van Bo Le-Mentzel, Rebecca Sandbichler,
Marie Voigt, Mathias Wetzl**

HATJE
CANTZ

Welcome!

This book is intended for the following four groups. Do you belong to one of these groups? Then go to the corresponding page:

1. DIY fans, page 27, 73
2. Interior design fans, page 11, 73
3. Start-ups and marketing managers, page 34, 48, 131
4. Communists and other crazy people, page 52, 115

I am the inventor of Hartz-IV-Möbel (German welfare furniture). Running a furniture-production business is very new for me. Completely without a factory or capital. With this do-it-yourself project, I put thousands of people to work without any overproduction occurring. Do it yourself (DIY) is the solution. Although no one is paid, everyone is highly motivated. After the furniture, now comes a book. Based on the same principle: designing not alone but together. Normally, an author comes up with a text, looks for a publisher, which then looks for readers. Generally, a book is first printed when it is finished. Here, everything is different. I started with selling. Amongst the so-called supporters, I found comrades-in-arms who wanted to write this book along with me. The book was created by the Crowd. That is what I call the many thousands of supporters of Hartz-IV-Möbel. This is a social DIY project that I initiated in 2010. An explanation: "Hartz IV" is the name of German welfare—a term that most German citizens deeply hate. The German word "Möbel" (furniture) derives from "mobile" and stands for what Germans love above everything else: architecture and lifestyle. The publisher came automatically, as did the money and the advertising in and around the project. I call this Karma Economy. But more on that later. Is this book intended only for poor people dependent on welfare? No, it is directed at all people with limited incomes and lots of taste. Why I chose this name is something

Willkommen!

Dieses Buch ist für folgende vier Gruppen gedacht. Findest Du Dich hier wieder? Dann spring zu den dahinter stehenden Seiten:

1. DIY-Fans, Seite 27, 73
2. Interior-Design-Fans, Seite 11, 73
3. Start-ups und Marketingmanager, Seite 34, 48, 131
4. Kommunisten und andere schräge Vögel, Seite 52, 115

Ich bin der Erfinder der Hartz-IV-Möbel. Das ist für mich ein neuartiges Prinzip, eine Möbelproduktion zu betreiben. Ganz ohne Fabrik und Kapital. Mit diesem Do-it-yourself-Projekt versetze ich Tausende von Menschen in Arbeit, ohne dass eine Überproduktion entsteht. Do it yourself (DIY) ist die Lösung. Obwohl niemand bezahlt wird, sind alle hoch motiviert. Nach den Möbeln kommt nun ein Buch. Nach dem gleichen Prinzip: Nicht allein, sondern gemeinsam gestalten. Normalerweise denkt sich ein Autor einen Text aus, sucht einen Verlag, der dann Leser sucht. In der Regel druckt man ein Buch erst, wenn es fertig ist. Hier ist alles anders. Ich habe angefangen mit dem Verkauf. Unter den sogenannten Supportern habe ich Mitstreiter gefunden, die dieses Buch mitschreiben wollen. Das Buch ist durch die Crowd entstanden. So nenne ich die vielen Tausend Unterstützer des Projektes Hartz-IV-Möbel. Das ist ein soziales DIY-Projekt, das ich 2010 initiiert habe. Zur Erklärung: Hartz IV ist der Name der deutschen Arbeitslosenhilfe – ein Wort, bei dem viele Ausschlag bekommen. Der Begriff Möbel stammt von mobil und steht für das, was die Deutschen über alles lieben: Architektur und Wohnen. Der Verlag kam wie von allein, das Geld und die Werbung drumherum auch. Ich nenne das Karma Economy. Dazu später mehr. Ist dieses Buch nur für Hartz-IV-Empfänger gedacht? Nein, es richtet sich an alle Menschen mit wenig Einkommen und viel Geschmack. Warum ich den Namen gewählt habe, erfährst Du auf den nächsten Seiten. Die Crowd besteht aus Erwerbslosen und

It takes 14 days and 1,400 euros to make Van Bo's Hartz-IV-Möbel Collection. From left to right / Es braucht 14 Tage und 1 400 Euro für Van Bos Hartz-IV-Möbel-Kollektion. Von links nach rechts: 2 x Kreuzberg-36-Chair, 1 x Piscator Table, 1 x SiWo-Sofa, 1 x Sideboard (6 Berliner Hocker), 1 x Coffee Table (2 Berliner Hocker), 1 x 24-Euro-Chair + 1 x TV-Board (3 Berliner Hocker)

that you will learn about in the pages that follow. The Crowd consists of people who are unemployed and people who earn money, young and old, healthy and ill, theorists and practical people, conservatives and visionaries. In an elevator, we would all turn away from each other. But what connects us is our position: constructing instead of consuming (build more, buy less). Do you like this approach? Then become part of the Crowd, since together we can make a big difference. For example, build new awesome chairs or take over the world …

From page 27 onward you will find instructions for building things, from a lamp to a bed. Here you will find the basics for your apartment, your office, or your school. All the designs are inspired by

Geldverdienern, Jungen und Alten, Gesunden und Kranken, Theoreti-
kern und Praktikern, Konservativen und Visionären. In einem Fahrstuhl
würden wir uns alle voneinander wegdrehen. Doch was uns verbindet,
ist unsere Haltung: konstruieren statt konsumieren (build more, buy
less). Gefällt Dir diese Einstellung? Dann werde Teil der Crowd, denn
gemeinsam können wir Großes bewirken. Zum Beispiel neue Möbel
bauen oder die Weltherrschaft an uns reißen ...

Ab Seite 27 findest Du Anleitungen von der Leuchte bis zum Bett.
Hier findest Du die Basics für Deine Wohnung, Dein Büro oder Deine
Schule. Alle Entwürfe sind von zeitlosen Klassikern der Moderne inspiriert und von der Crowd ständig weiterentwickelt worden. Deshalb entwickeln sich auch die Baupläne immer weiter. Du kannst die aktuelle

timeless modern classics and have been continuously further developed by the Crowd. This is why the building plans also continue to develop. You can request the current versions of the building plans on my website. Free of charge. So that your personal building project does not disappear into a drawer, we have come up with an idea: take a hole punch and press it where there are two points marked in black. You can then nail your favorite project to the wall. And when you have built it, I would enjoy receiving a photo of you and your work! The current building plans are available here: www.hartzivmoebel.com

Yours truly,
Van Bo Le-Mentzel and the Crowd

Bauplanversion auf meiner Webseite anfordern. Kostenfrei. Damit Dein persönliches Bauprojekt nicht in der Schublade verschwindet, haben wir uns etwas ausgedacht: Nimm einen Locher und drück ihn an die beiden schwarz markierten Stellen. Dann kannst Du Dein Lieblingsprojekt an die Wand nageln. Und wenn Du es geschafft hast, freue ich mich über ein Foto von Dir und Deinem Werk! Aktuelle Baupläne gibt es hier: www.hartzivmoebel.com

Dein Van Bo Le-Mentzel und die Crowd

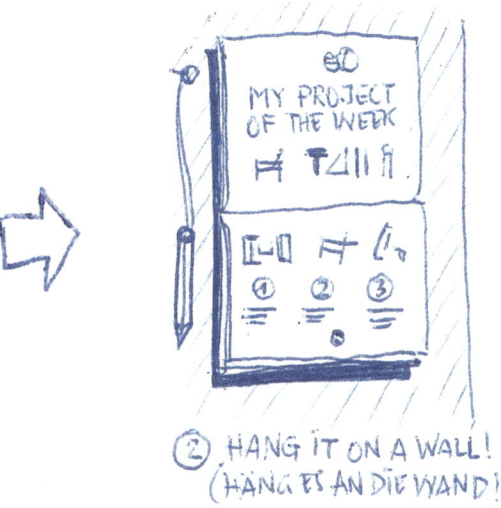

9

Deep orange / Tieforange –
approx. / etwa RAL 2011

Perfect for the more hidden spaces within furniture, for
example in the Beta Block, the Berliner Hocker, and the Neukoelln Desk / Perfekt für Möbelinnenseiten, beispielsweise für
den Beta Block, den Berliner Hocker und den Neukoelln Desk

inter
view

An interview with Van Bo Le-Mentzel with Rebecca
Sandbichler; revised version of the interview,
published in *NEON* magazine, **May 2012** / Van Bo
Le-Mentzel im Interview mit Rebecca Sandbichler;
überarbeitete Version des Interviews, erschienen in der
Zeitschrift *NEON*, Mai 2012

Illustrations / Illustrationen:
Bruno Miguel Fernandes Maltez
Photos / Fotos:
Kay Strasser, Emrullah Gümüşsoy

"Furniture Should Make You Horny"

Rebecca Sandbichler: **In my hand, a hammer risks causing injury. Can I still build your furniture anyway?**

Van Bo Le-Mentzel: **Of course, I was terrible at working with my hands myself. I created my first chair because of a wounded sense of honor. I finally wanted to show myself that I, too, could build something. Normally, I am more the type who tries to solve things with his head. When faced with a loose door handle, I still get the jitters today. But there comes a point in life when one has to show that he is a man by using a hammer and a saw.**

Rebecca: **So you went to adult education classes in a quite manly way?**

Van Bo: **Adult education classes naturally have an uncool image. But for learning carpentry, the workshop was ideal. Anyway, as an incompetent person, I did manage to build my own chair there within twenty-four hours. And it even has a tongue-and-groove joint. Such things are usually only done by real carpenters, not laypeople. That's why I was also really proud of the 24-Euro-Chair and showed it on the Internet.**

Rebecca: **In the meantime, people worldwide have reproduced it and you get several hundred inquiries each day. Why should people self-build furniture when it's less expensive to buy it at IKEA?**

Van Bo: **For me, do it yourself expresses the general spirit of the times. We ask ourselves where our food comes from, why a T-shirt costs only 5 euros, and who earned money from it. The best way to understand these complex questions a little bit better is to make things yourself. People no longer want to eat what is put in front of them in the shop. That's why the interest in this chair was so big. For me it's important to discuss this Do-It-Yourself project in a**

»Möbel müssen Lust auf Sex machen«

Rebecca Sandbichler: Ein Hammer wird in meiner Hand zum Verletzungsrisiko. Kann ich trotzdem Deine Möbel bauen?

Van Bo Le-Mentzel: Natürlich, ich war selbst eine handwerkliche Niete. Mein erster Stuhl ist aus verletztem Ehrgefühl entstanden. Ich wollte mir endlich beweisen, dass auch ich etwas bauen kann. Normalerweise bin ich nämlich eher der Typ, der Dinge mit dem Kopf zu lösen versucht. Vor einer lockeren Türklinke habe ich auch heute noch Bammel. Aber es kommt der Moment im Leben, da muss man mit dem Hammer und der Säge zeigen, dass man ein Mann ist.

Rebecca: Also bist Du ganz männlich in die Volkshochschule gegangen?

Van Bo: Die Volkshochschule hat natürlich ein uncooles Image. Aber um das Tischlern zu lernen, war die Werkstatt ideal. Immerhin habe ich als Nichtskönner dort innerhalb von 24 Stunden einen eigenen Stuhl gebaut. Und der hat sogar eine Fingerverzinkung. So etwas machen eigentlich nur richtige Tischler, keine Laien. Darum war ich auch mächtig stolz auf den 24-Euro-Chair und habe ihn im Internet hergezeigt.

Rebecca: Er wird inzwischen von Leuten aus der ganzen Welt nachgebaut, mehrere Hundert Anfragen kriegst Du am Tag. Doch warum wollen die Menschen selbst Möbel bauen, wenn es bei IKEA doch immer noch günstiger geht?

Van Bo: Do it yourself ist für mich ein Ausdruck für den allgemeinen Zeitgeist. Wir fragen uns, wo unser Essen herkommt, warum ein T-Shirt nur 5 Euro kostet und wer dabei verdient hat. Die beste Möglichkeit, um diese komplexen Fragen ein bisschen besser zu verstehen, ist Selbermachen. Die Menschen wollen nicht mehr fressen, was

way that's socio-critical. Living is a social issue for me, and not exclusively an issue of design. That's why I wanted to find the most asocial word in Germany: Hartz IV. This is what our unemployment and social welfare system is called. Whoever googles "Hartz IV" in Germany probably has a lot of problems. It's these people I'd like to reach, and not only handyman fans.

Rebecca: And do you think you reach them?

Van Bo: Thousands of my followers are unemployed or seriously ill. But also a lot of them are burn-out patients or pensioners or single mothers. We're a diverse bunch. What connects us is the belief that it is better to build more and buy less.

Rebecca: Your share your building plans with anyone who is interested and also accept the fact that they will be altered.

Van Bo: I'm even happy about it. Because that way, the designs constantly improve. People write me that the armrests are too thin or that the straps are too loose. From the first model, we're now already at Version 3.0.

Rebecca: But people don't get your plans for free. Everyone has to fill out a form with questions.

Van Bo: The people's stories are my remuneration. I love these stories, am virtually addicted to them. But people also get something in return: they receive applause for their completed project and a platform on my website. And in the best case, it also changes their lives a bit because they become mobile: they have to spend time in a workshop and buy the wood. Or people that they have not talked to for ten years call and ask to borrow their saw. This is an important part of the concept.

Rebecca: What kinds of people request your plans?

Van Bo: Quite of few of them are in a phase of transition: the student who now has his or her own apartment, the woman who has separated from her partner, a couple moving to a new city. They feel the need to mark the new beginning with a successful project. And the furniture that they have built will always remind them of this exciting time.

ihnen im Laden vorgesetzt wird. Deshalb war wohl das Interesse für diesen Stuhl so groß. Mir ist dabei wichtig, dass dieses Do-it-yourself-Projekt sozialkritisch diskutiert wird. Wohnen ist für mich ein soziales Thema und kein reines Designthema. Deshalb habe ich das asozialste Wort Deutschlands gesucht: Hartz IV. So heißt in Deutschland unsere Arbeitslosenhilfe. Wer in Deutschland nach »Hartz IV« googelt, hat vermutlich viele Sorgen. Diese Menschen wollte ich erreichen. Nicht nur die Heimwerkerfans.

R e b e c c a : Und erreichst Du sie?

V a n   B o : Tausende meiner Follower sind arbeitslos oder dauerhaft krank. Aber auch viele Burnout-Patienten, Rentner und alleinerziehende Mütter sind dabei. Wir sind sehr unterschiedlich. Was uns eint, ist der Glaube, dass es besser ist, zu konstruieren statt zu konsumieren.

R e b e c c a : Du teilst Deine Baupläne mit allen Interessierten und nimmst auch in Kauf, dass sie verändert werden.

V a n   B o : Ich freue mich sogar darüber. Denn so werden die Entwürfe laufend verbessert. Die Leute schreiben mir, dass die Armlehnen zu dünn sind oder der Gurt zu locker. Vom ersten Modell gibt es mittlerweile schon die Version 3.0.

R e b e c c a : Man kriegt Deine Pläne aber nicht umsonst. Jeder muss ein Formular mit Fragen beantworten.

V a n   B o : Die Geschichten der Leute sind meine Bezahlung. Ich liebe diese Geschichten, ich bin regelrecht süchtig nach ihnen. Dafür bekommen die Menschen aber auch etwas von mir: Sie kriegen Applaus für ihr fertiges Projekt und eine Plattform auf meiner Webseite. Und im besten Fall verändert sich auch ihr Leben ein bisschen, weil sie mobil werden: Sie müssen eine Werkstatt suchen und das Holz kaufen. Oder Leute, mit denen sie seit zehn Jahren nicht gesprochen haben, anrufen und nach ihrer Säge fragen. Das ist ein wichtiger Teil des Konzepts.

R e b e c c a : Was sind das für Menschen, die Deine Pläne anfordern?

V a n   B o : Ganz viele sind in einer Umbruchphase: Der Student, der jetzt eine eigene Wohnung hat. Die Frau, die sich von ihrem Freund getrennt hat. Ein Paar, das in einer neuen Stadt zusammenzieht. Die

Rebecca: **Why should people be so proud of a chair?**

Van Bo: **The Bauhaus director Ludwig Mies van der Rohe once said that it is more difficult to build a good chair than a skyscraper. And it's true. Because a high-rise building often only consists of a floor plan that is multiplied many times over. In the case of a chair, it's a question of every detail. Nothing can be concealed. The design is pure.**

Rebecca: **Your designs are especially purist. And there's lots of Bauhaus in them.**

Van Bo: **That's something that I actually didn't become aware of until later. In the case of my first chair, I didn't want to spend more than 20 euros or have to build for a long time, nor did I want to use a lot of wood because I didn't have a car to transport it. So I ended up at the essentially German Bauhaus ideals.**

Rebecca: **Many of your pieces of furniture can be taken onto the subway after they have been assembled. Why it that so important?**

Van Bo: **We need furniture that corresponds to our lives. And our lives have become global and mobile. People think about whether they should study in Frankfurt, work in Munich, live in New York, or perhaps do an internship in Japan.**

Our whole biography doesn't really follow a straight line: education, job, marrying, starting a family, dying. It's all intertwined, and that's why furniture also has to cooperate.

Rebecca: **The self-built stool for one's whole life?**

Van Bo: **When everything around us is virtual and on the move, we need things that ground us and that are enduring. That's also why I love wood so much. In my designs, I take care that they are "grandchild-proof." The children of your children should be able to sit on a stool at some point and know that their grandmother built it.**

Rebecca: **You have also invented the so-called "Guerilla Lounging." What exactly is that?**

Van Bo: **From time to time, I put a call out to the Crowd via Facebook to make a public space cozy. It might be a subway station, an**

haben das Bedürfnis, den Neuanfang mit einem erfolgreichen Projekt zu markieren. Und das Möbel, das sie gebaut haben, wird sie immer an diese aufregende Zeit erinnern.

Rebecca: Warum darf man auf seinen Stuhl so stolz sein?

Van Bo: Der Bauhaus-Direktor Ludwig Mies van der Rohe hat einmal gesagt, es sei schwerer, einen guten Stuhl zu bauen als einen Wolkenkratzer. Und das stimmt. Denn ein Hochhaus besteht oft einfach nur aus einem vervielfachten Grundriss. Bei einem Stuhl geht es aber um jedes Detail. Nichts lässt sich verstecken, das Design ist pur.

Rebecca: Deine Entwürfe sind besonders puristisch. Und überall steckt Bauhaus drin.

Van Bo: Das ist mir eigentlich erst hinterher bewusst geworden. Bei meinem ersten Stuhl wollte ich nicht viel mehr als 20 Euro ausgeben, nicht lange bauen müssen und nicht viel Holz verwenden, weil ich kein Auto für den Transport hatte. So landete ich bei den urdeutschen Idealen des Bauhaus.

Rebecca: Manche Deiner Möbel kann man zusammengebaut in die U-Bahn mitnehmen. Warum ist das so wichtig?

Van Bo: Wir brauchen Möbel, die unserem Leben entsprechen. Und das ist global und mobil geworden. Die Leute überlegen, ob sie in Frankfurt studieren, in München arbeiten, in New York leben oder vielleicht in Japan ein Praktikum machen sollen.

Unsere ganze Biografie ist nicht so geradlinig: Ausbildung, Job, Heiraten, Familie gründen, Sterben. Das alles geht ineinander über, und deshalb müssen auch die Möbel das mitmachen.

Rebecca: Der selbstgebaute Hocker für das ganze Leben?

Van Bo: Wenn alles um einen herum virtuell und in Bewegung ist, braucht man Dinge, die einen erden und die Bestand haben. Darum liebe ich auch Holz so sehr. Ich achte bei meinen Entwürfen darauf, dass sie »enkeltauglich« sind. Die Kinder Deiner Kinder sollen irgendwann auf einem Hocker sitzen und wissen, den hat Oma gebaut.

Rebecca: Du hast auch das sogenannte Guerilla Lounging erfunden. Was genau ist das?

Van Bo: Von Zeit zu Zeit rufe ich die Crowd auf, einen öffentlichen

Guerilla Lounging Airport Tegel. **Organized by** / Organisiert von **Marco Spies, Victoria Mackintosh, and** / und **Hans Pul**

elevator at an airport, or the waiting area of a city hall. Many take it as a joke. In reality, however, I am pursuing two goals. First, to draw attention to spaces that, in my opinion, deserve more attention because of their architectural quality. And second, to create a location where I can exchange ideas with my Crowd.

R e b e c c a : **Your motto is also "build more, buy less." Is this position something that is left over from the time when you were dependent on social benefits yourself?**

V a n B o : **For me, it wasn't that bad. I fled with my parents from Laos and came to Germany and wasn't familiar with prosperity. But how we live naturally depends on money: how much space we have, which district we live in, how it smells on the street corner there. All this has a profound effect. Depending on how much a person has, that person also dreams of other things. We, for example, had a picture of a palm-lined beach on fake, wooden wallpaper. Because we thought that wood paneling was something for rich people.**

R e b e c c a : **Most people don't really live the way they dream of living. What horrible furniture do you see quite often?**

Occupy subway station / U-Bahnstation **"Kreuzberg"**:
Marie Voigt, Van Bo, and / und **Chris Doering**

Raum gemütlich zu machen. Das kann ein U-Bahnhof, ein Fahrstuhl im Flughafen oder eine Wartehalle im Rathaus sein. Viele halten das für einen Scherz. In Wirklichkeit verfolge ich damit zwei Ziele: erstens Aufmerksamkeit auf Räume lenken, die meiner Meinung nach aufgrund ihrer architektonischen Qualität mehr Aufmerksamkeit verdienen. Und zweitens einen Ort schaffen, an dem ich mich mit meiner Crowd austauschen kann.

R e b e c c a : Dein Motto ist auch »konstruieren statt konsumieren«. Ist Dir diese Einstellung aus der Zeit geblieben, in der Du selbst von Sozialleistungen abhängig warst?

V a n B o : Für mich war das nicht schlimm. Ich bin mit meinen Eltern von Laos nach Deutschland geflohen und kannte keinen Wohlstand. Aber vom Geld hängt natürlich die Wohnsituation ab: Wie viel Platz hat man, in welchem Viertel lebt man, wie riecht es da an der Straßenecke? Das ist sehr prägend. Je nachdem, wie viel man hat, träumt man aber auch von anderen Dingen. Wir hatten zum Beispiel ein Bild von einem Palmenstrand auf einer Fake-Holztapete. Weil wir dachten, Holzvertäfelungen wären etwas für reiche Leute.

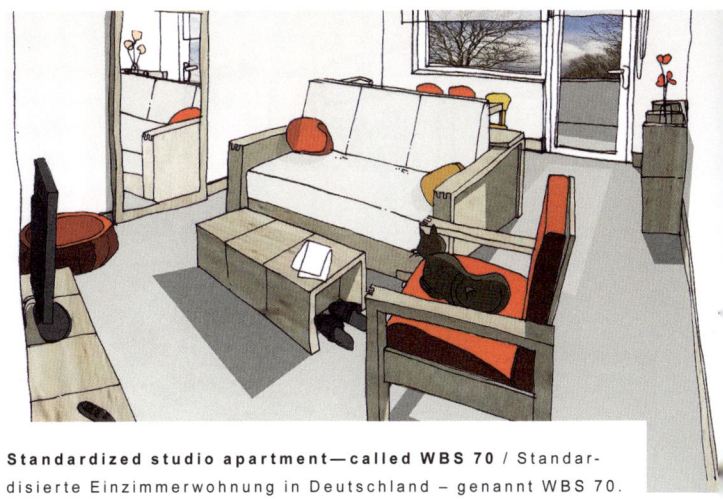

Standardized studio apartment—called **WBS 70** / Standardisierte Einzimmerwohnung in Deutschland – genannt WBS 70.

Van Bo: **There are trends that people run after even when they have nothing to do with their own personal reality. For example, the huge sofa, also called a seating landscape. This useless monstrosity is supposed to say: "I'm an incredibly urban type and live in a converted factory building. That's why I also have an incredibly large sofa." But in reality, only very few people live in such a loft. It's more likely that people are living in a WBS 70.**

Rebecca: **What's that?**

Van Bo: **The "Wohnbauserie 70," or residential housing series 70 in the former German Democratic Republic, the most common type of prefabricated building in Germany. People who don't have much money, including many students, live in such apartments. The one-room apartments have a living space measuring around 20 square meters. An XXL seating landscape just doesn't fit. Or it does, but then you don't have a table anymore. And that means that you can't invite your parents over for Easter dinner.**

Rebecca: **So when in doubt, always choose the table?**

Van Bo: **You have to consider what your needs are. And since**

R e b e c c a : Die meisten leben ja nicht so, wie sie es sich erträumen. Welche schrecklichen Möbel siehst Du ganz oft?

V a n   B o : Es gibt Trends, denen die Menschen hinterherrennen, auch wenn sie mit ihrer Realität nichts zu tun haben. Zum Beispiel das riesige Sofa; man nennt es auch Sitzlandschaft. Diese nutzlosen Ungetüme sollen sagen: »Ich bin ein wahnsinnig urbaner Typ und lebe in einer ausgebauten Fabrikhalle. Darum habe ich auch ein wahnsinnig großes Sofa.« In Wahrheit leben aber die wenigsten Leute in so einem Loft. Viel eher wohnen sie in einer WBS 70.

R e b e c c a : Was ist das?

V a n   B o : Die Wohnbauserie 70 der ehemaligen DDR, der am weitesten verbreitete Plattenbautyp Deutschlands. Menschen mit wenig Geld und auch viele Studenten leben in solchen Wohnungen. Die Einzimmerapartments haben einen Wohnraum von etwa 20 Quadratmetern. Da passt keine XXL-Sitzlandschaft rein. Oder schon, aber dann hat man keinen Tisch mehr. Und das heißt, dass man seine Eltern nicht zum Osteressen einladen kann.

R e b e c c a : Also im Zweifel immer den Tisch wählen?

most people want to have a social life, it makes sense to have a large table.

Rebecca: You have also solved another classic problem of students: bed or sofa?

Van Bo: In the best case, both in one. But people don't sleep very well on most sofa beds because they don't have a slatted frame. Or the sleeping comfort is okay, but they don't have any armrests. Have you ever tried making out on a sofa without armrests? You fall off to the sides. That is hostile to procreation. Furniture has to be inviting. It should make you horny.

Rebecca: Is your SiWo-Sofa suitable for sex?

Van Bo: It is a sofa bed with a slatted frame and armrests for making out. So yes. But it's also possible to use the backside as bench seating.

Rebecca: It's typical for your designs to have various functions.

Van Bo: The more multifaceted the furniture is, the better. For an apartment is supposed to offer you something: having fun, procreating, cooking, and inviting friends to eat. Furniture should make all of this possible and not inhibit it.

Rebecca: If someone wants to work, eat, sleep, have parties and sex in one room, what should they do?

Van Bo: What's important is to have zones for the various functions of the apartment. They have to be staged really well, for instance with a striking pendant luminaire. Carpet and rugs are also really good for delimiting areas. And what I have also recognized: in small apartments, large pieces of furniture are not a problem in and of themselves as long as they are positioned correctly.

Rebecca: And how exactly?

Van Bo: The largest piece of furniture has to be in the middle, and not everything should be put up against a wall. This means that you are forced to walk around the furniture and automatically change your perspectives more often. Your brain appreciates more of the areas in the room and thinks: wow, so many impressions, it really is absolutely huge in here.

Van Bo: Man muss sich überlegen, welche Bedürfnisse man hat. Und da die meisten Leute soziale Kontakte wollen, ist es sinnvoll, einen großen Tisch zu haben.

Rebecca: Du hast noch ein klassisches Studentenproblem gelöst: Bett oder Sofa?

Van Bo: Am besten beides in einem. Allerdings schläft man auf den meisten Sofas nicht gut, weil sie keinen Lattenrost haben. Oder der Schlafkomfort stimmt, aber sie haben keine Armlehnen. Hast Du schon mal probiert, auf einem Sofa ohne Armlehnen zu knutschen? Man fällt auf den Seiten runter. Das ist fortpflanzungsfeindlich. Ein Möbel muss einladend sein. Man soll Lust auf Sex bekommen.

Rebecca: Dein SiWo-Sofa ist sextauglich?

Van Bo: Es ist ein Bettsofa mit Lattenrost und Lehnen zum Knutschen. Also ja. Man kann die Rückseite aber auch an einem Tisch als Sitzbank verwenden.

Rebecca: Die vielen Funktionen sind ja typisch für Deine Entwürfe.

Van Bo: Je vielseitiger die Möbel, desto besser. Denn die Wohnung muss Dir Angebote machen: Dass Du Spaß hast, Dich vermehrst, kochst und Freunde zum Essen einlädst. Möbel sollten all das ermöglichen und nicht verhindern.

Rebecca: Wenn man in einem Raum Arbeiten, Essen, Schlafen, Feiern und Sex haben will: Wie sollte man vorgehen?

Van Bo: Wichtig sind Zonen für die verschiedenen Funktionen der Wohnung. Man muss sie richtig schön inszenieren, zum Beispiel mit einer auffälligen Pendelleuchte. Auch Teppiche sind sehr gut geeignet, um Bereiche abzugrenzen. Und was ich noch erkannt habe: In kleinen Wohnungen sind große Möbel an sich kein Problem, solange man sie richtig platziert.

Rebecca: Und zwar wie?

Van Bo: Das größte Möbel muss in die Mitte, man sollte nicht alles an die Wand stellen. Dadurch ist man nämlich gezwungen, um Möbel herumzulaufen und wechselt automatisch öfter die Perspektive. Das Gehirn nimmt mehrere Bereiche des Zimmers wahr und denkt: Wow, so viele Eindrücke, ist ja bestimmt total riesig hier.

Rebecca: But don't people already trip over enough stuff in students' rooms?

Van Bo: Naturally, there should simply be less stuff, especially in small apartments. Tiny living spaces are indeed a problem of city dwellers. That's why they should also adapt to the city and take advantage of the local infrastructure, meaning, preferably go to the supermarket more often instead of getting a huge refrigerator.

Rebecca: What else can I do to feel more comfortable in my apartment?

Van Bo: The most important thing is to accept the identity of the place. In a new building with low-ceilings, you shouldn't act as if it were a hundred-year-old building. The architect wanted people to live there in a modern manner and horizontally. You can, of course, still integrate ornate country house furniture, but it will always feel somehow inconsistent.

Rebecca: Your designs continue to develop in an evolutionary way. Is this also how people should furnish their apartments: slowly?

Van Bo: Definitely. Many things are impossible to plan in advance: How does the light come through the window in the morning? Where do the neighbors have their bathroom? Are there places where the floor always squeaks? Or do I intuitively have a favorite spot? It's better not to rush, but to be daring and always try out new things.

Rebecca: What did you first have to learn about furnishing apartments yourself?

Van Bo: In the past, I aped other people's styles. If I liked a page in the IKEA catalogue, I bought it exactly that way. In the meantime I know that you have to surround yourself with the things that you love. Not with things for which you hope to get recognition. It doesn't matter if there is a kitschy Hello Kitty blanket on your couch. If it makes you happy because your friend gave it to you, use it and stand behind it.

R e b e c c a : Stolpert man in Studentenzimmern nicht schon über genug Kram?

V a n   B o : Natürlich sollte man gerade in kleinen Wohnungen einfach weniger Zeug haben. Winziger Lebensraum ist ja ein Städterproblem. Darum sollten sie sich auch an die Stadt anpassen und die örtliche Infrastruktur nutzen. Also lieber öfter in den Supermarkt gehen, statt einen riesigen Kühlschrank zu besorgen.

R e b e c c a : Was kann ich noch tun, um mich in meiner Wohnung wohler zu fühlen?

V a n   B o : Vor allem muss man die Identität des Ortes akzeptieren. In einem niedrigen Neubau sollte man nicht so tun, als wäre es ein Jahrhundertwendehaus. Der Architekt wollte, dass man modern und horizontal darin lebt. Natürlich kann man trotzdem verschnörkelte Landhausmöbel reinstellen, es wird sich aber immer irgendwie widersprüchlich anfühlen.

R e b e c c a : Deine Entwürfe entwickeln sich evolutionär weiter. Sollte man auch seine Wohnung so einrichten: langsam?

V a n   B o : Unbedingt. Vieles kann man vorher gar nicht planen: Wie fällt das Licht morgens durchs Fenster? Wo haben die Nachbarn ihr Badezimmer? Gibt es Stellen am Boden, die immer knirschen? Oder habe ich intuitiv einen Lieblingsplatz? Man sollte lieber nichts überstürzen. Aber schon mutig sein und immer wieder neue Dinge ausprobieren.

R e b e c c a : Was hast Du selbst erst über Einrichtung lernen müssen?

V a n   B o : Früher habe ich fremde Stile nachgeäfft. Hat mir eine Seite im IKEA-Katalog gefallen, habe ich sie genau so nachgekauft. Inzwischen weiß ich, dass man sich mit den Dingen umgeben muss, die man liebt. Nicht mit Sachen, von denen man sich Anerkennung erhofft. Es ist egal, wenn auf deiner Couch eine kitschige Hello-Kitty-Decke liegt. Wenn sie dich glücklich macht, weil du sie von deinem Freund bekommen hast: Verwende sie und steh dazu.

Gray white / Grauweiß –
approx. / etwa RAL 9002

Perfect for offices and the SiWo-Sofa / Perfekt für Büros und
das SiWo-Sofa

Do it your self

**DIY for Amateurs with a
Low Income but Great Taste**

DIY für Amateure mit wenig Geld,
aber gutem Geschmack

Design / Entwurf: **Van Bo Le-Mentzel**
Illustrations / Illustrationen:
**Fine Heininger, Alessa Joosten, Alexandra Kahl,
Van Bo Le-Mentzel, Carolina López Tomás,
Hoang Hoa Nguyen, Nele Ouwens, Sandra
Schauer, Sabine Schmidt, Tammo Winkler**

24
euro
chair

24 € + cushions / Kissen

24 hours / Stunden

Difficulty level / Schwierigkeitsgrad **++**

W x D x H / B x T x H: **60 x 60 x 66 cm**

Illustration (on this spread / auf dieser

Doppelseite): **Alessa Joosten**

Inspiration

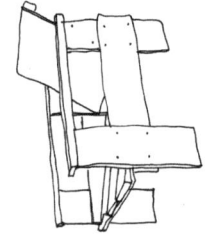

Crate Chair
1934
Gerrit Rietveld

Barcelona Chair MR 90
1929
Ludwig Mies van der
Rohe

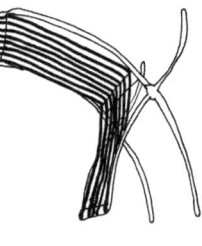

Armchair / Armlehnen-
stuhl
Ca. 1926
Erich Dieckmann

Wassily Chair B 3
1925
Marcel Breuer

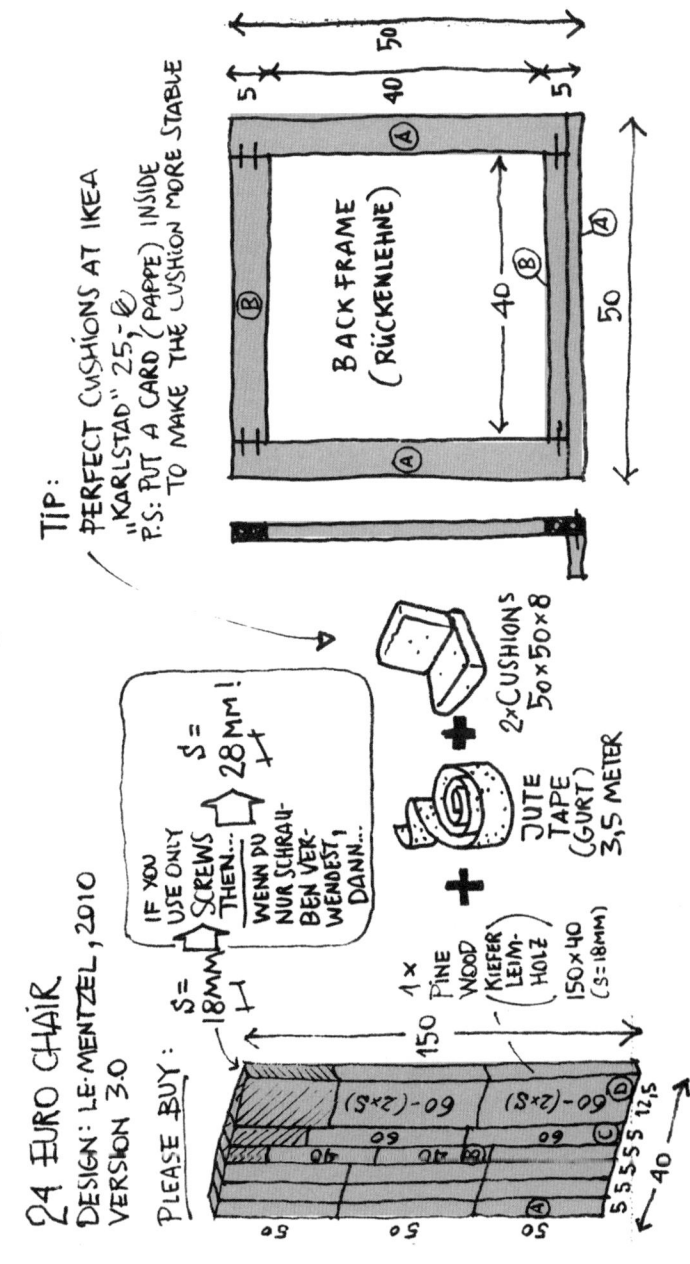

24 EURO CHAIR
DESIGN: LE·MENTZEL, 2010
VERSION 3.0

TIP:
- PERFECT CUSHIONS AT IKEA
  "KARLSTAD" 25,- €
  P.S: PUT A CARD (PAPPE) INSIDE
  TO MAKE THE CUSHION MORE STABLE

BACK FRAME
(RÜCKENLEHNE)

50
5   40   5
40
50

A   A   A   B   B

2× CUSHIONS
50×50×8

JUTE
TAPE
(GURT)
3,5 METER

IF YOU
USE ONLY
SCREWS
THEN...
WENN DU
NUR SCHRAU-
BEN VER-
WENDEST,
DANN...
S =
28 MM!

S =
18 MM

PLEASE BUY:

1 ×
PINE
WOOD
(KIEFER
LEIM-
HOLZ)
150×40
(S=18MM)

150
60-(2×S)
60-(2×S)
60
60
40 40 40
50
50
50
5 5 5 5 5 12,5
40
A C D

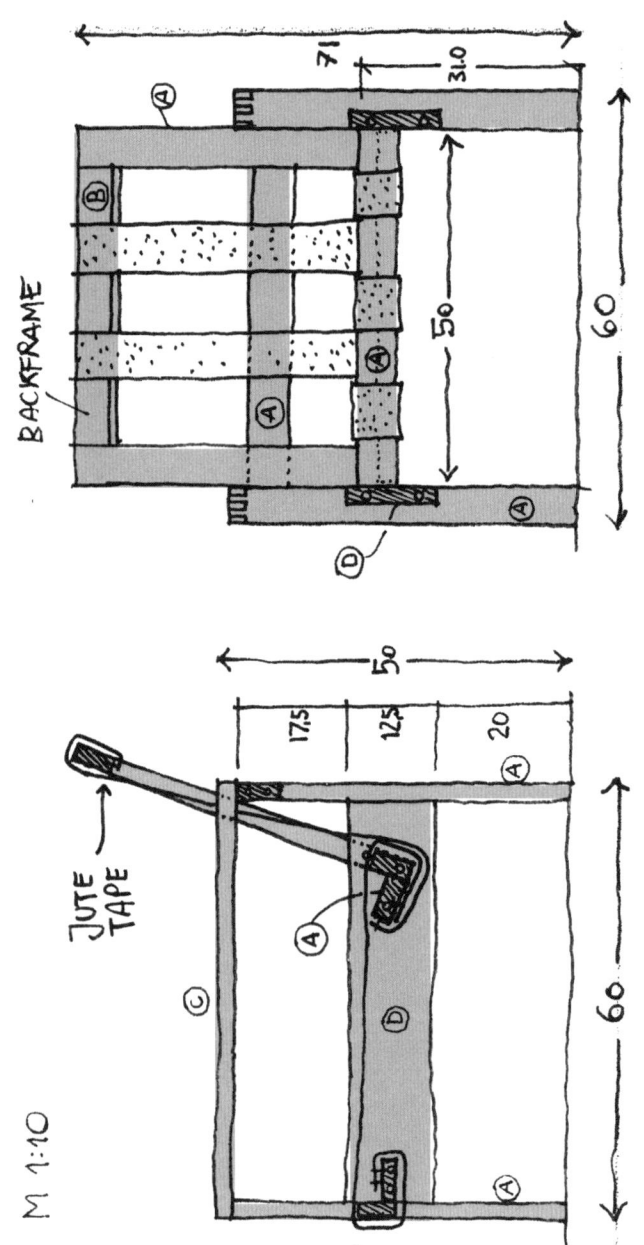

M 1:10

JUTE TAPE

BACKFRAME

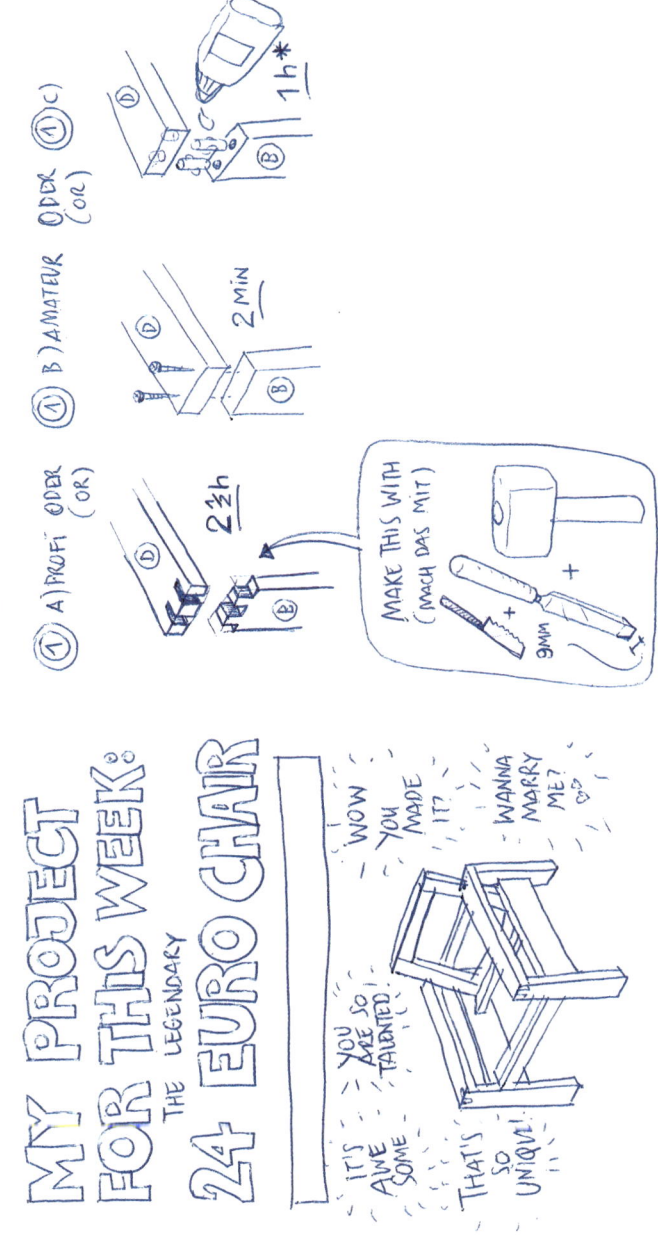

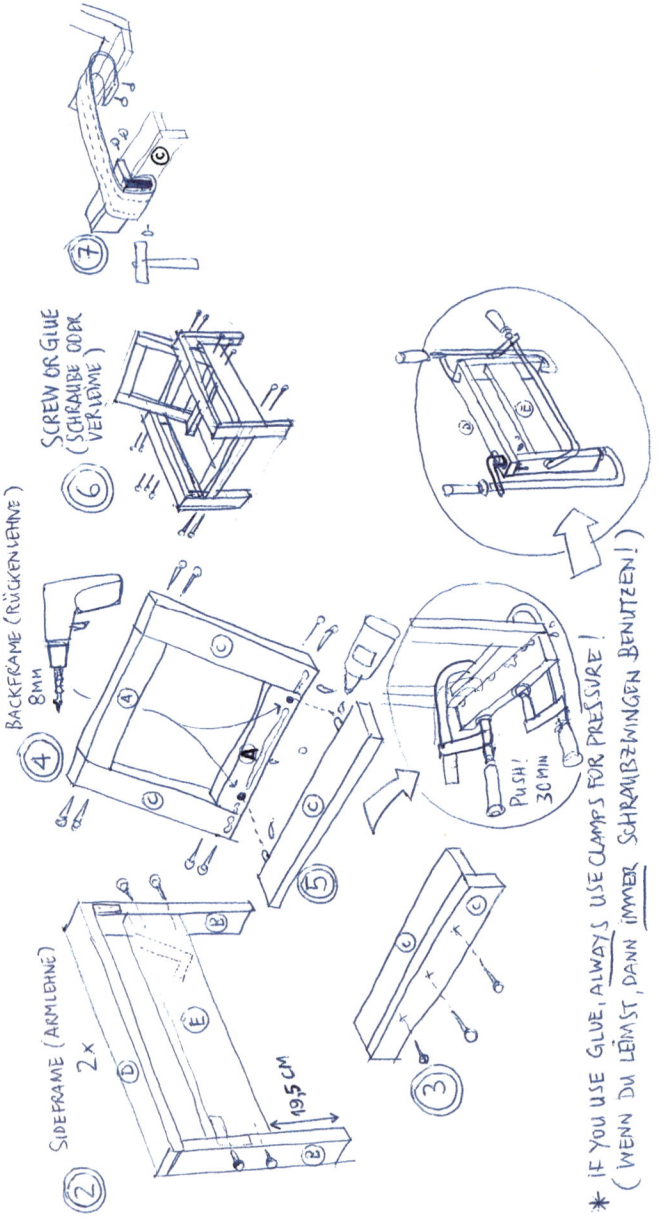

② SIDEFRAME (ARMLEHNE)
2×

19,5 CM

③

④ BACKFRAME (RÜCKENLEHNE)
8MM

⑤

PUSH!
30 MIN

⑥ SCREW OR GLUE
(SCHRAUBE ODER
VERLEIME)

⑦

* IF YOU USE GLUE, ALWAYS USE CLAMPS FOR PRESSURE!
(WENN DU LEIMST, DANN IMMER SCHRAUBZWINGEN BENUTZEN!)

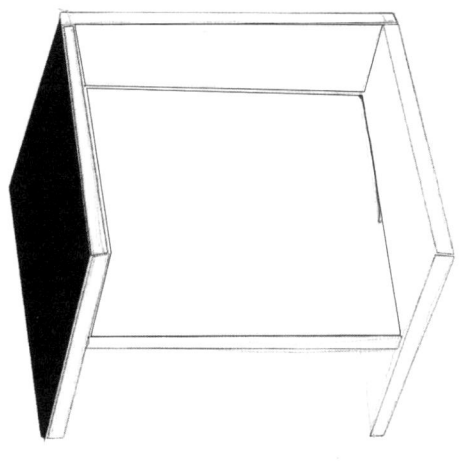

berliner
hocker

10 €

10 screws / Schrauben

10 minutes / Minuten

Difficulty level / Schwierigkeitsgrad +

W x D x H / B x T x H: 30 x 32 x 47 cm

Illustration (on this spread / auf dieser Doppelseite): Alexandra Kahl

Inspiration

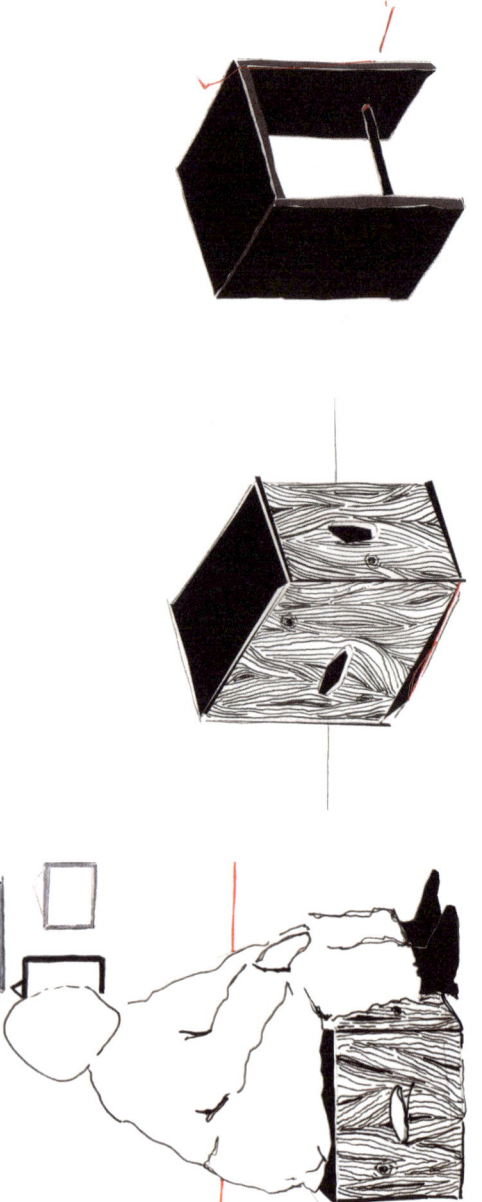

"Itten-Hocker"
1930
Johannes Itten

LC 14
1952
Le Corbusier

Ulmer Hocker
1954
Max Bill

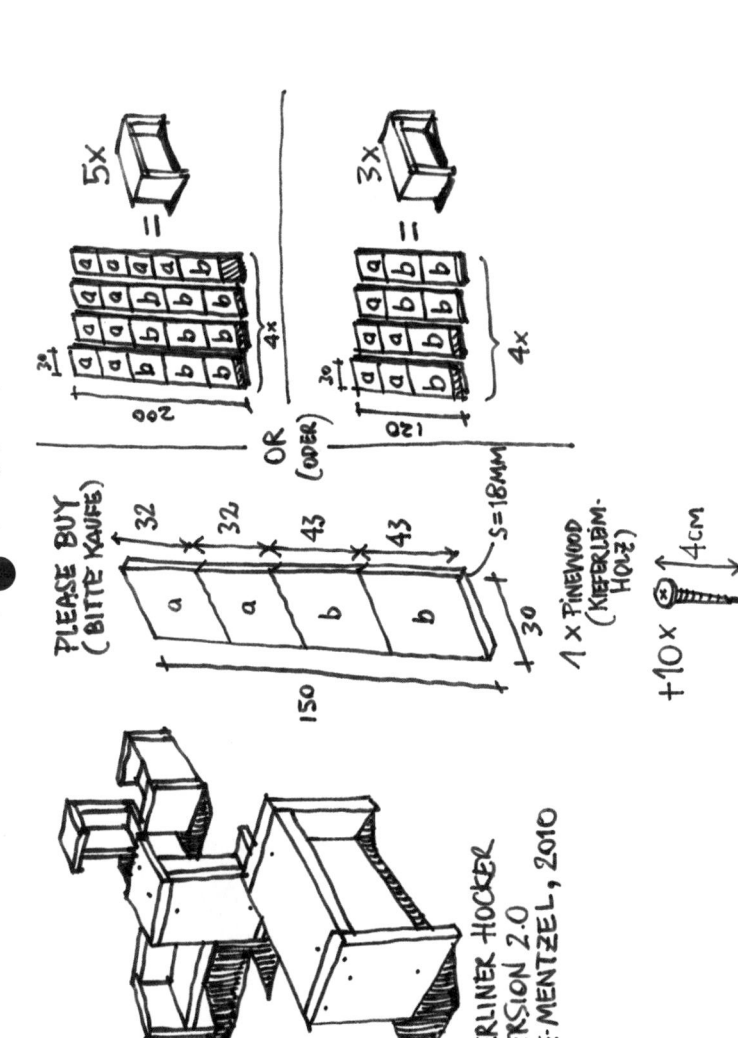

PLEASE BUY
(BITTE KAUFEN)

5x =

3x =

OR
(ODER)

a a b b

150

32 32 43 43

S=18MM

30

1 x PINEWOOD
(KIEFERLEIM-
HOLZ)

+ 10x   4CM

BERLINER HOCKER
VERSION 2.0
LE-MENTZEL, 2010

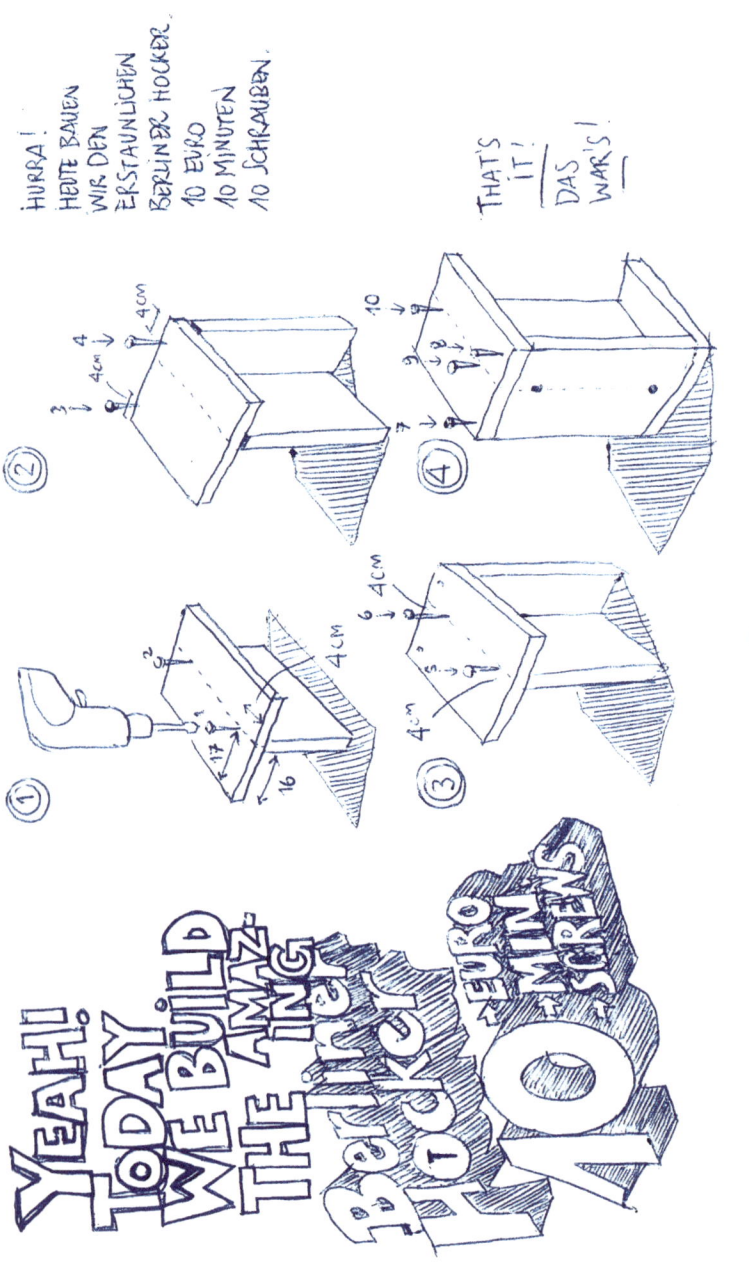

YEAH! TODAY WE BUILD THE AMAZING

Berlicky Hocker

10 EURO ↑ 10 MINS ↑ 10 SCREWS

HURRA!
HEUTE BAUEN
WIR DEN
ERSTAUNLICHEN
BERLINER HOCKER.
10 EURO
10 MINUTEN
10 SCHRAUBEN.

THAT'S IT!
DAS WAR'S!

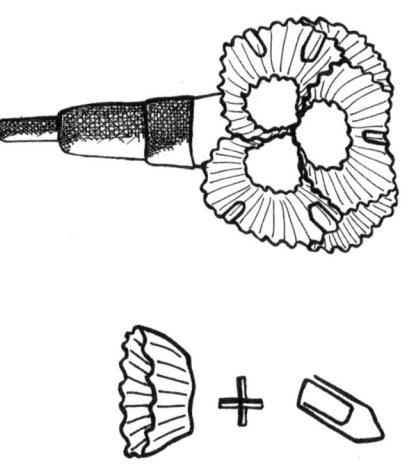

100 sec lamp

100 cents / Cents

100 seconds / Sekunden

Difficulty level / Schwierigkeitsgrad +

Diameter / Durchmesser: **ca. 18 cm**

Illustration (on this spread / auf dieser Doppelseite): **Nele Ouwens**

Take approx. 12 muffin cups and attach them to an energy-saving light bulb with 3 to 5 paper clips each. Don't worry: muffin cups can withstand high temperatures. If making a large lamp, then wrap tape around the cups to give them extra strength. / Nimm etwa 12 Muffincups und klemme sie mit 3 bis 5 Büroklammern pro Muffinpapier um eine Sparlampe. Keine Sorge: Muffinpapier hält hohe Temperaturen aus. Bei größeren Lampen wickle Tesastreifen um die Cups, um sie zu stärken.

Inspiration

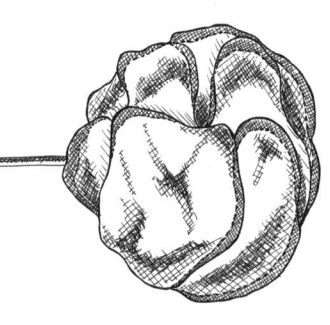

Cloud Suspension Light
Fixture
2005
Frank O. Gehry

"Dandelion Seed" Lamp /
»Pusteblumen«-Leuchter
Humboldt-Universität zu
Berlin
1960s / 1960er-Jahre
VEB Leipziger Werke,
Leuchtenbau

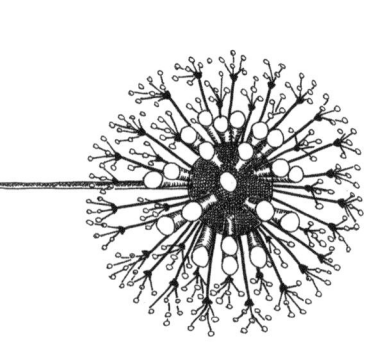

"Dandelion Seed" Lamp /
»Pusteblumen-Leuchter«
Leipziger Oper
1961
VEB Leipziger Werke,
Leuchtenbau

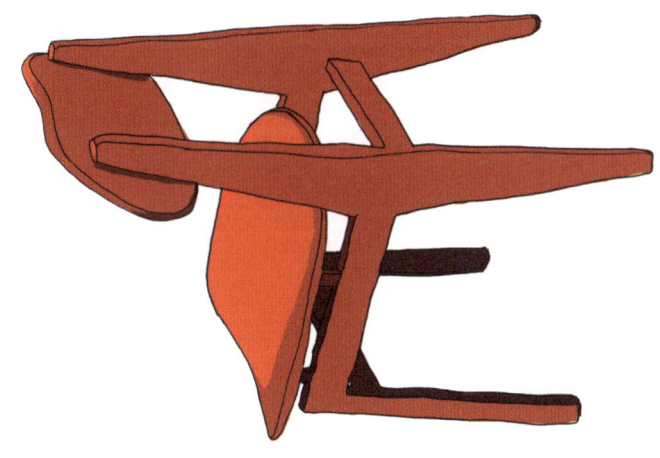

kreuz
berg 36
chair

36 €

36 hours / Stunden

Difficulty level / Schwierigkeitsgrad **+++**

W x D x H / B x T x H: 47 x 52 x 81 cm

SH: 43–47 cm

Illustration (on this spread / auf dieser Doppelseite): Hoang Hoa Nguyen

Inspiration

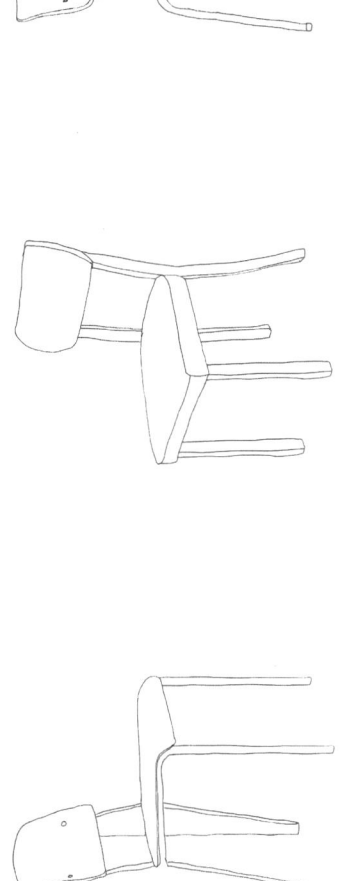

Standard Chair
1934
Jean Prouvé

Frankfurt Kitchen Chair /
Frankfurter Küchenstuhl
1935
Max Stoeckler

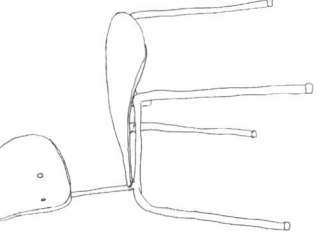

Chair SE 68
1950
Egon Eiermann

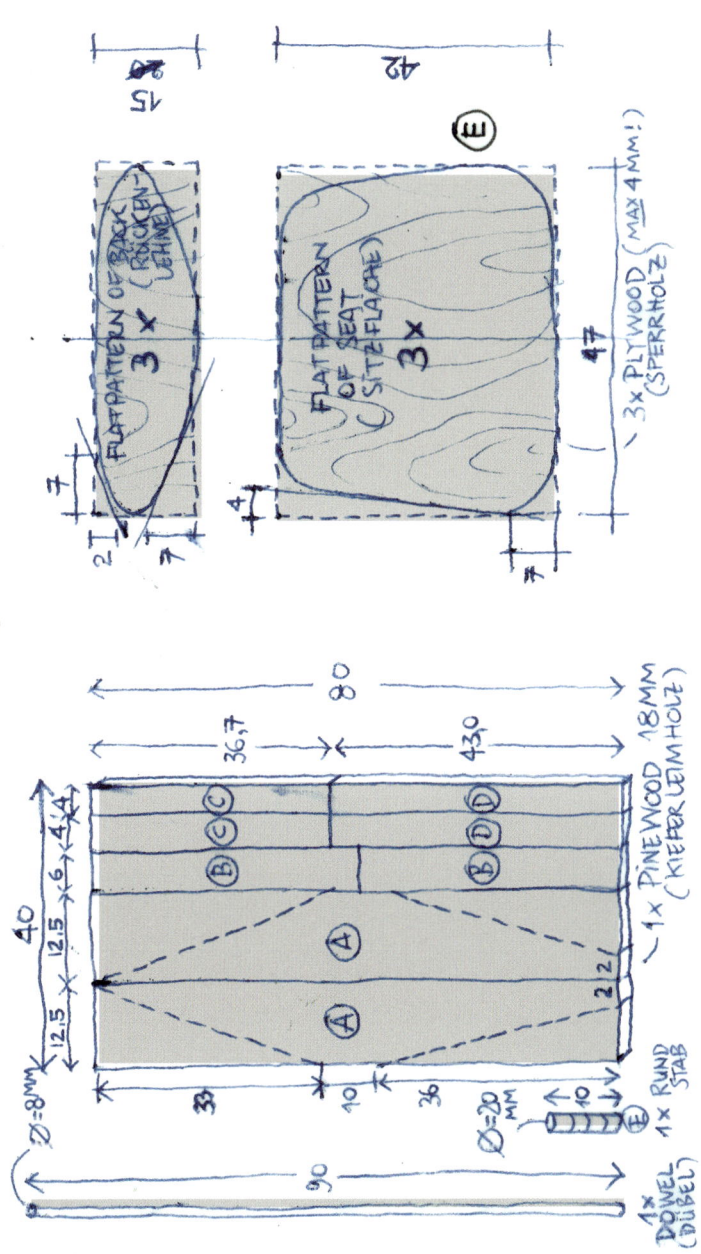

Flat pattern of back (Rücken-lehne) 3×

Flat pattern of seat (Sitzfläche) 3×

3× Plywood (max 4mm!) (Sperrholz)

15
8

42

47

7
7
2
7

4

4

Ⓜ

80

36,7   43,0

40

12,5 × 6 × 4'A'

Ⓑ Ⓒ Ⓒ

Ⓑ Ⓓ Ⓓ

Ⓐ

Ⓐ

12,5 × 12,5

∅ = 8mm

1× Pinewood 18mm (Kiefer Leimholz)

33   10   36

22

∅ = 20mm

10

Ⓔ

1× Rund Stab

90

1× Dowel (Dübel)

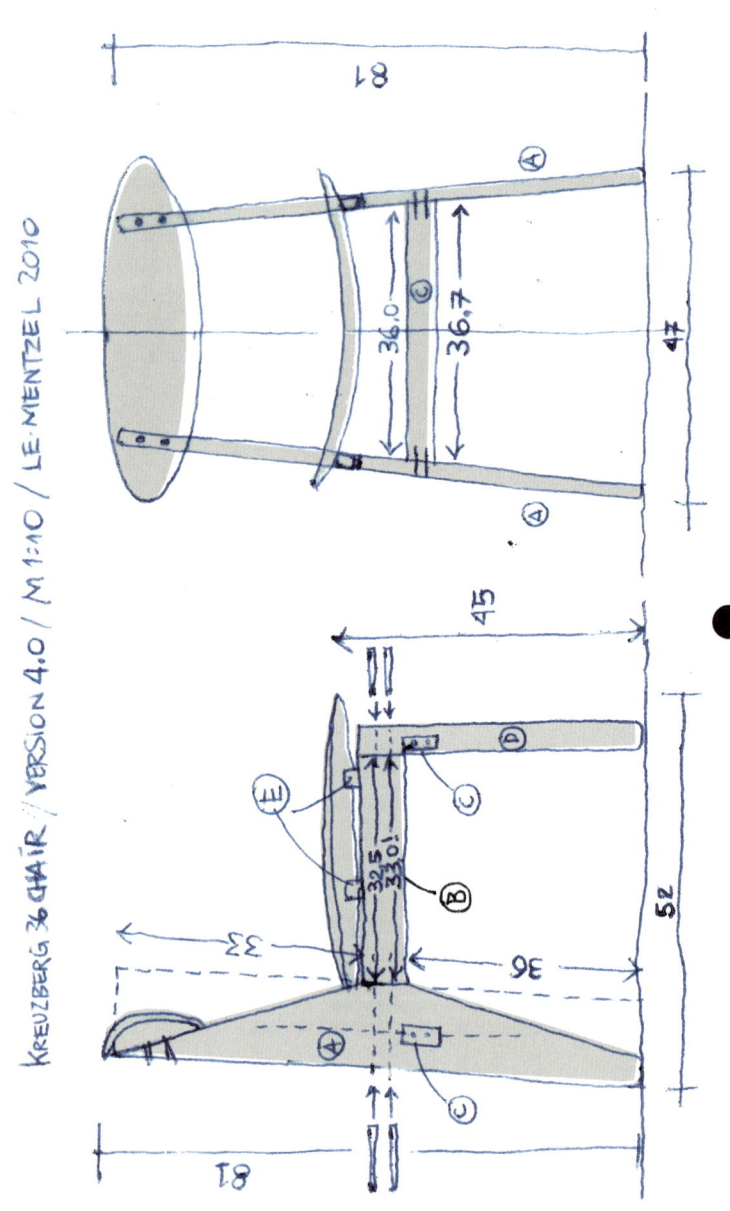

KREUZBERG 36 CHAIR // VERSION 4.0 / M 1:10 / LE·MENTZEL 2010

81

47

36,0
36,7

Ⓐ
Ⓐ
Ⓒ

45

52

81

33

36

Ⓔ
Ⓒ
Ⓑ
Ⓓ
Ⓒ
Ⓐ

32,5
33,0

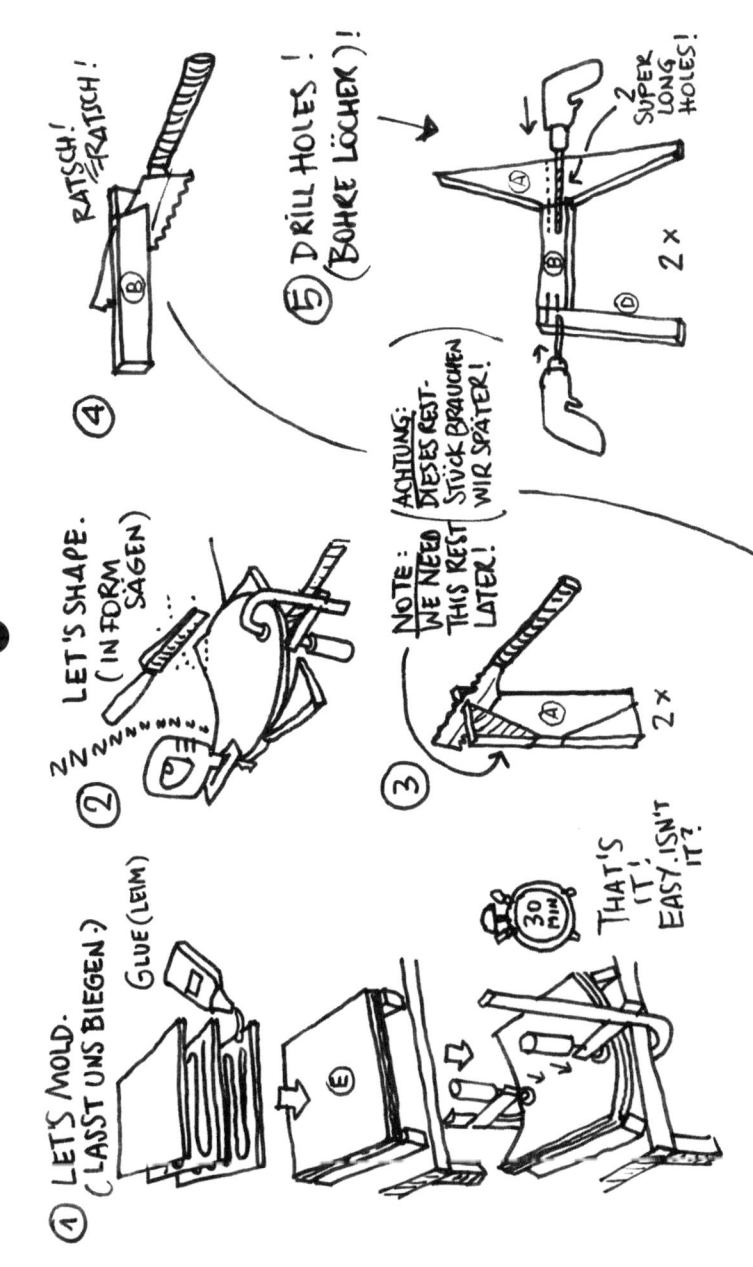

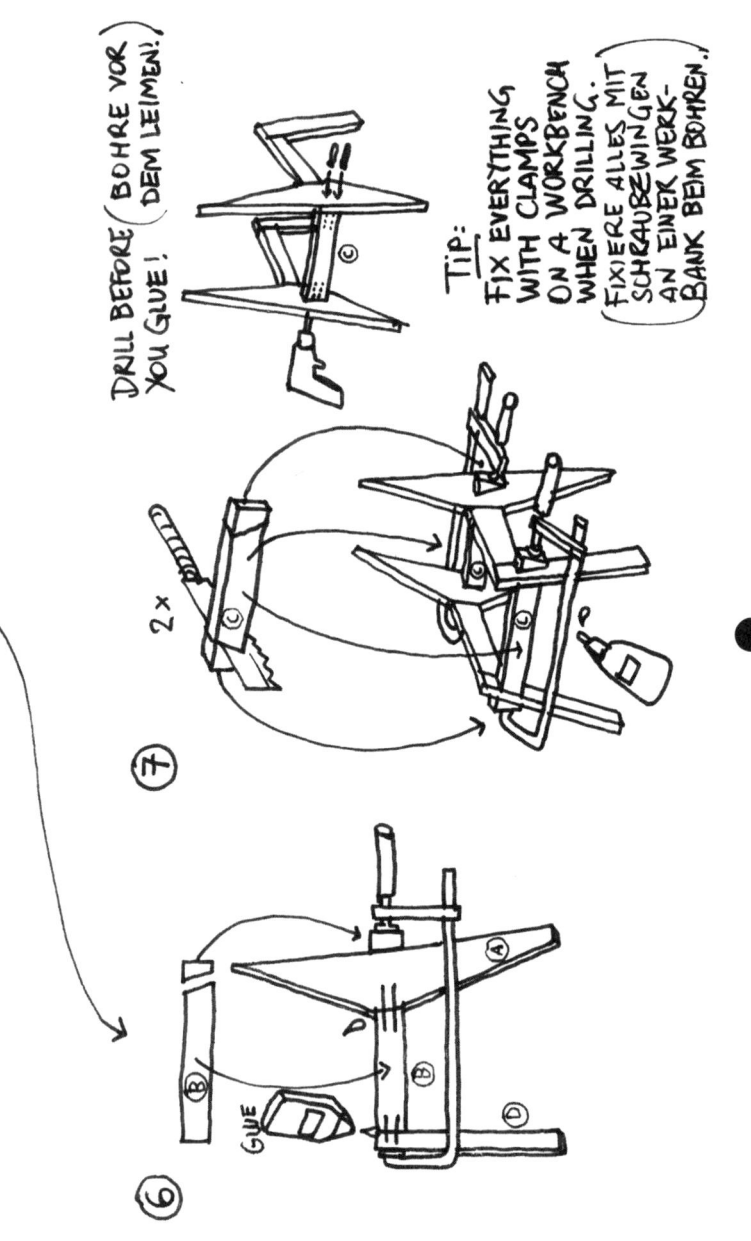

DRILL BEFORE (BOHRE VOR
YOU GLUE! DEM LEIMEN!)

TIP:
FIX EVERYTHING
WITH CLAMPS
ON A WORKBENCH
WHEN DRILLING.

(FIXIERE ALLES MIT
SCHRAUBZWINGEN
AN EINER WERK-
BANK BEIM BOHREN.)

2×

GLUE

Ⓐ
Ⓑ
Ⓒ
Ⓓ

⑥
⑦

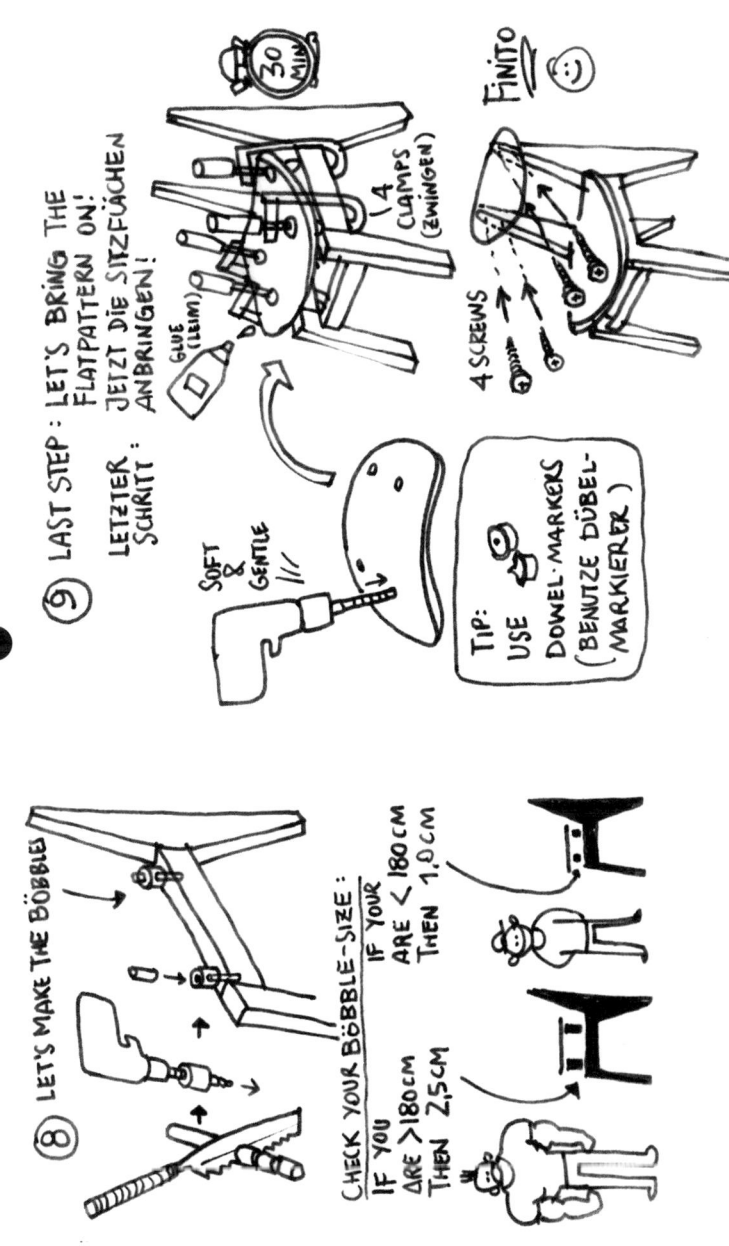

⑨ LAST STEP : LET'S BRING THE FLATPATTERN ON!
JETZT DIE SITZFLÄCHEN ANBRINGEN!

LETZTER SCHRITT

30 MIN

GLUE (LEIM)

4 CLAMPS (ZWINGEN)

FINITO :)

4 SCREWS

SOFT & GENTLE

TIP: USE DOWEL-MARKERS (BENUTZE DÜBEL-MARKIERER)

⑧ LET'S MAKE THE BÖBBLES

CHECK YOUR BÖBBLE-SIZE :

IF YOU ARE > 180CM THEN 2,5CM

IF YOU ARE < 180 CM THEN 1,0 CM

CHOOSE YOUR SHAPE (WÄHLE DEINE FORM):

M 1:10

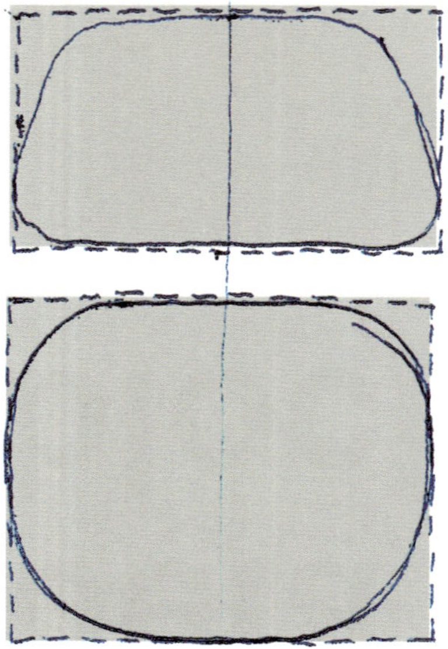

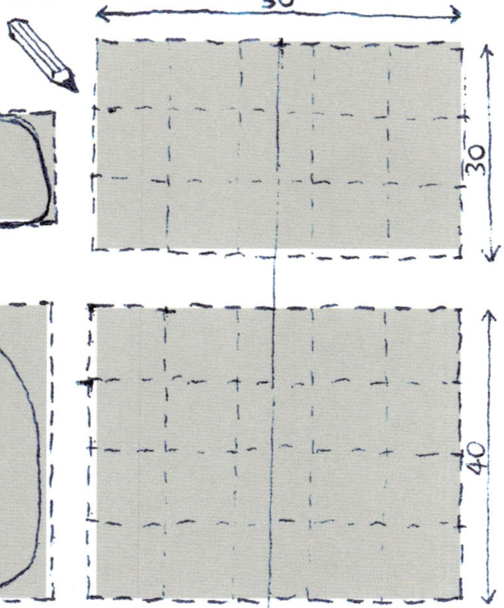

YOUR STYLE → [F]

FRANKFURT STYLE

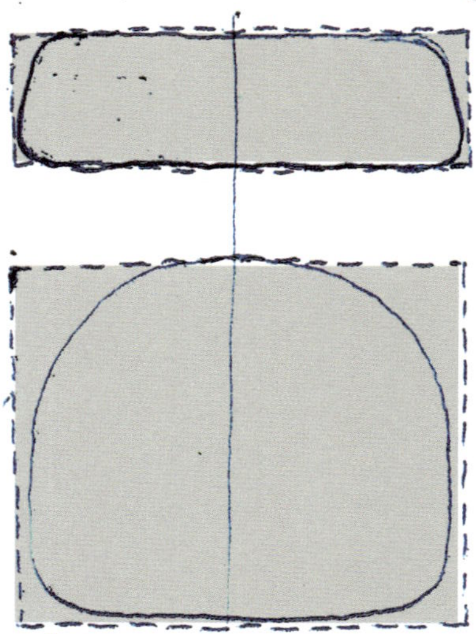

CALIFORNIA STYLE

30

40

50

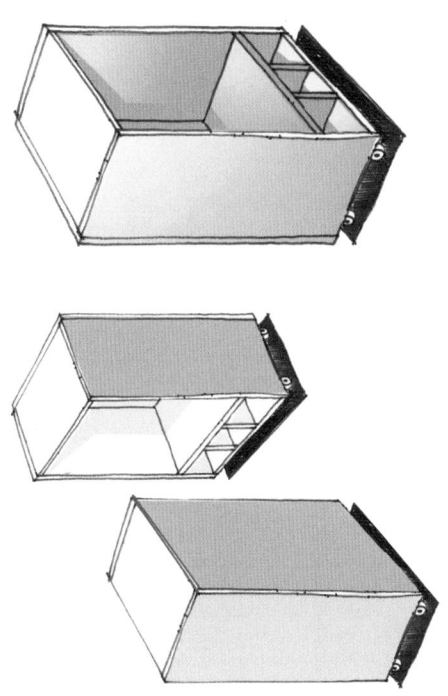

beta
block

200 €

2 days / Tage

Difficulty level / Schwierigkeitsgrad **++**

W x D x H / B x T x H: **30 x 32 x 47 cm**

Illustration (on next page / auf folgender

Seite): **Fine Heininger**

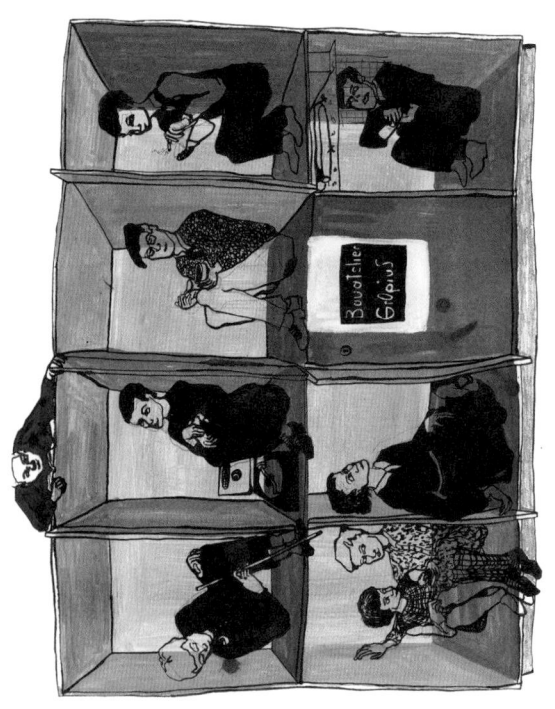

From the Gropius studio /
Aus dem Atelier Gropius

1928

Walter Gropius

Inspiration

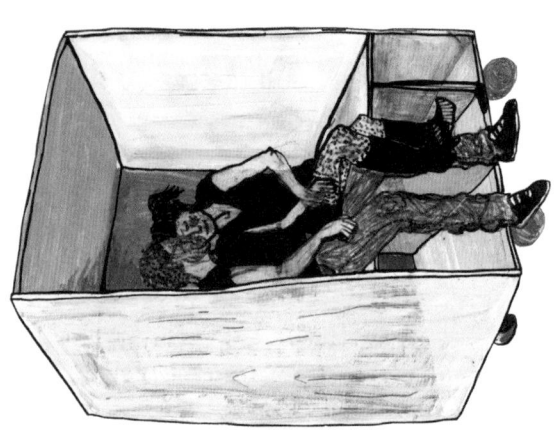

LET'S BUILD IT!

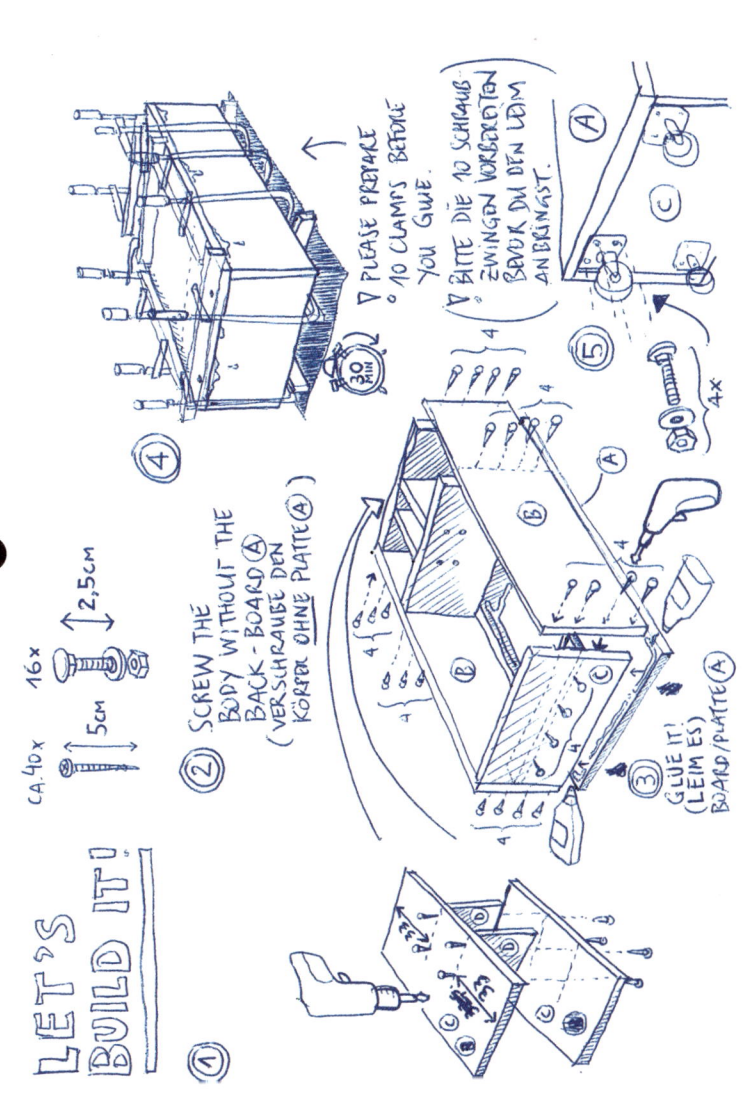

CA. 40x
16x

⟂ 5cm
↕ 2,5cm

①

② SCREW THE BODY WITHOUT THE BACK-BOARD Ⓐ
(VERSCHRAUBE DEN KÖRPER OHNE PLATTE Ⓐ)

③ GLUE IT! (LEIM ES) BOARD/PLATTE Ⓐ

④

⑤

⟐ PLEASE PREPARE
∘ 10 CLAMPS BEFORE YOU GLUE.

⟐ BITTE DIE 10 SCHRAUB-ZWINGEN VORBEREITEN BEVOR DU DEN LEIM ANBRINGST.

30 MIN

4x

Ⓐ Ⓑ Ⓒ

WELCHER BETA TYP BIST DU? WHICH BETA-TYPE ARE YOU!

- ☐ MESS!
- ☐ SALES-MANAGER
- ☐ FASHION-VICTIM
- ☐ BARKEEPER
- ☐ SHOWGIRL
- ☐ ARTIST

PISCATOR TABLE

pis
cator
table

120 €

12 hours / Stunden

Difficulty level / Schwierigkeitsgrad ++

W x D x H / B x T x H: 120–180 x 80 x 73 cm

Illustration (on this spread / auf dieser

Doppelseite): **Carolina López Tomás**

Inspiration

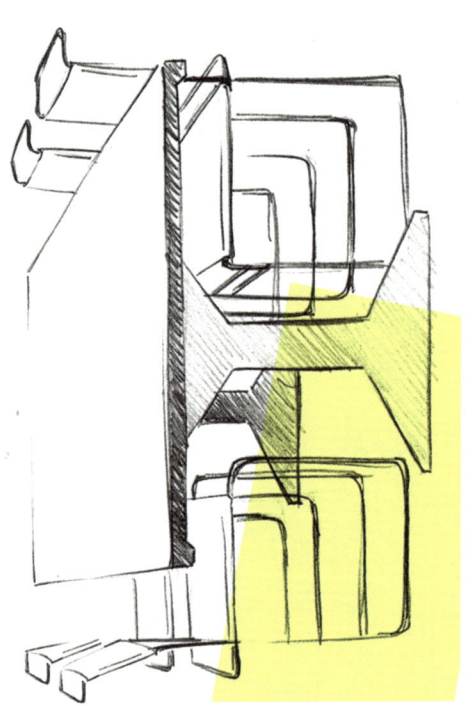

Table for Erwin Piscator /
Tisch für Erwin Piscator

1927

Marcel Breuer

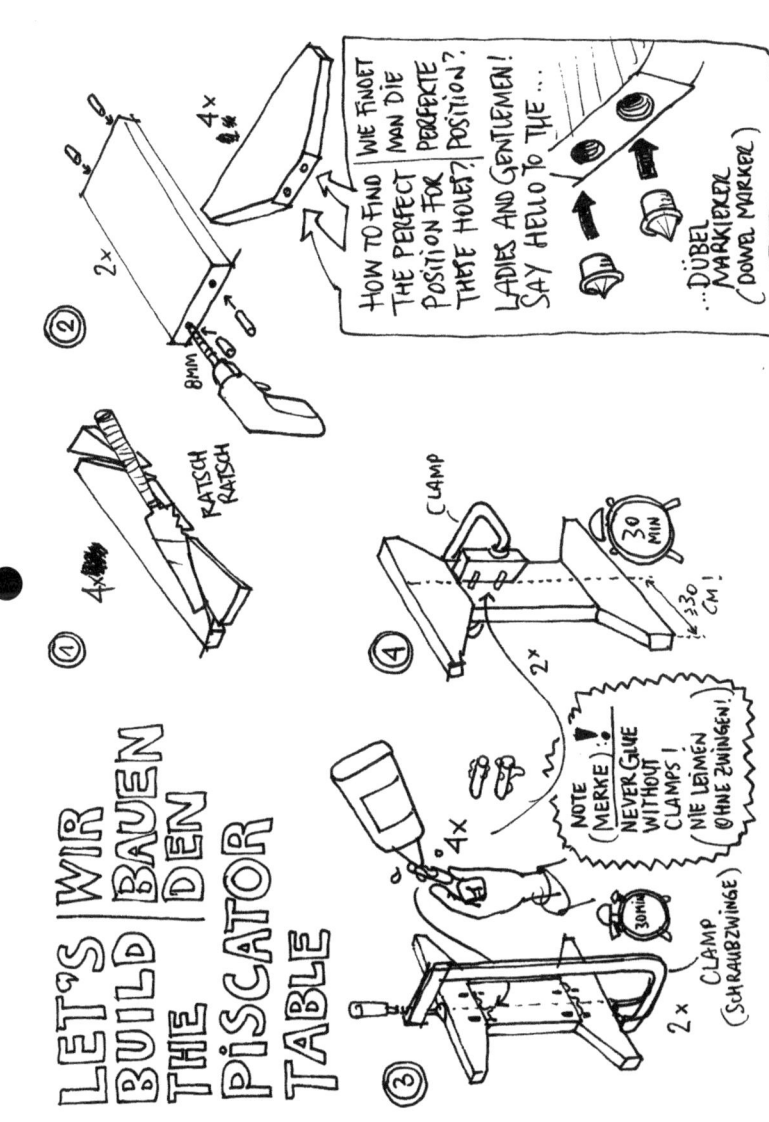

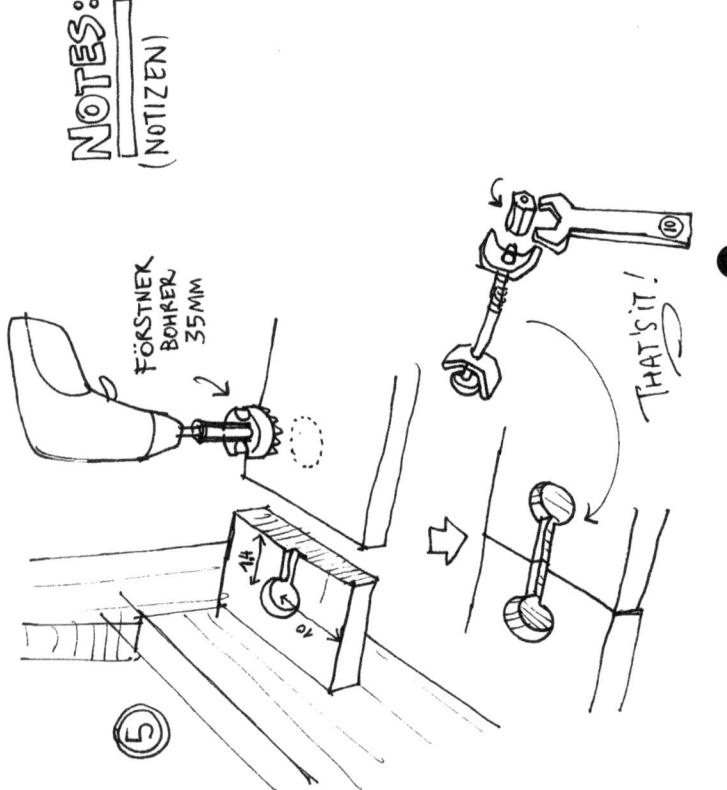

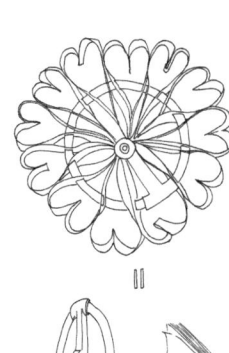

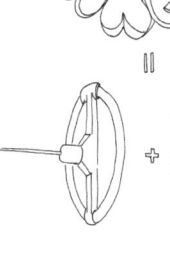

neon
hearts
lamp

20 €

20 minutes / Minuten

Difficulty level / Schwierigkeitsgrad +

Diameter / Durchmesser: **ca. 42 cm**

Illustration (on this spread / auf dieser

Doppelseite): **Sandra Schauer**

Inspiration

NEON (100th edition
issued in 2012 / 100.
Ausgabe von 2012).
magazine / Zeitschrift

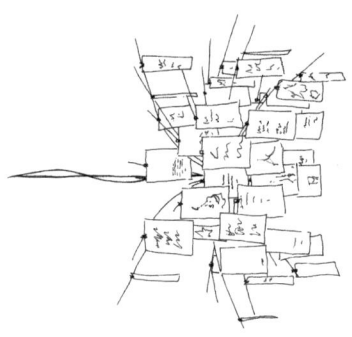

Zettel'z
1997
Ingo Maurer

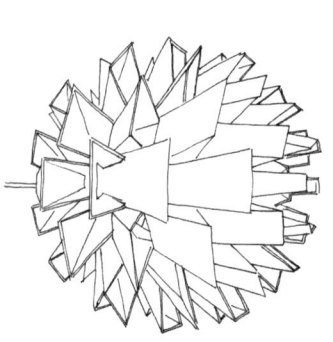

Norm 69
1969
Simon Karkov

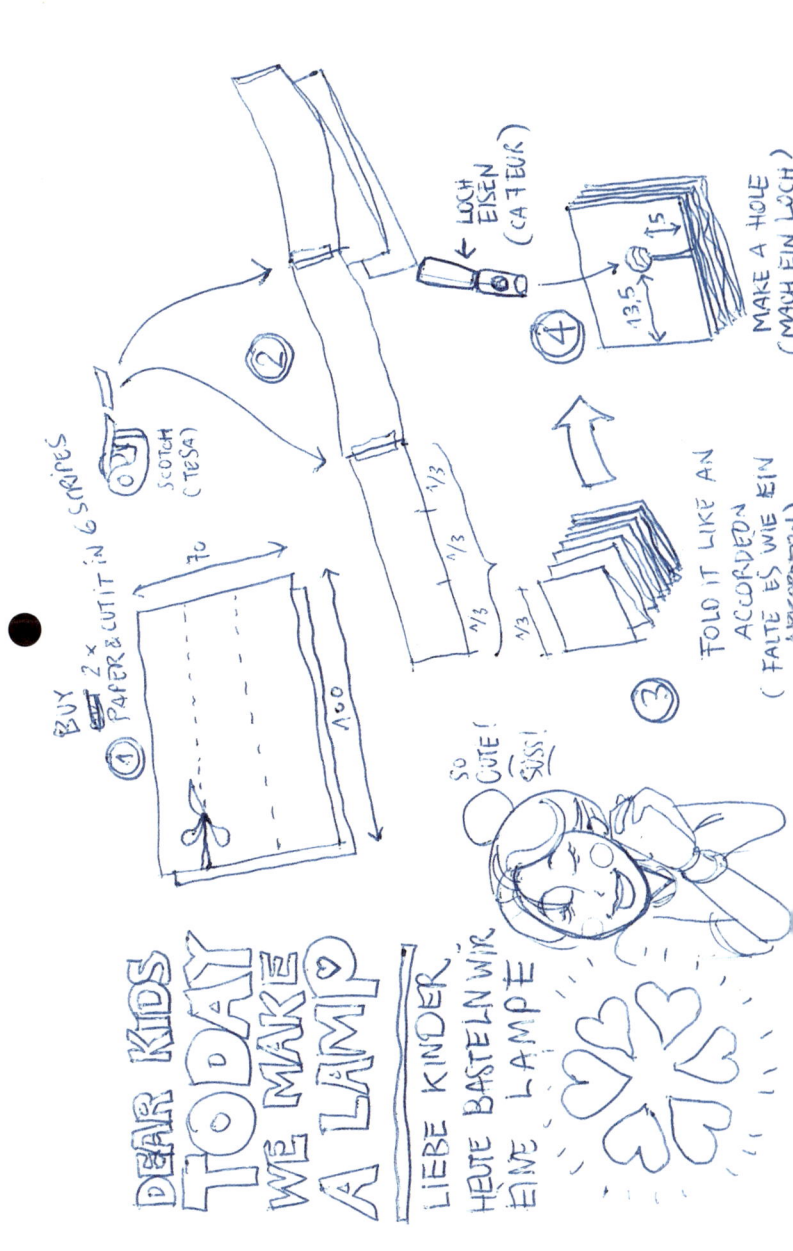

DEAR KIDS
TODAY
WE MAKE
A LAMP ♥

LIEBE KINDER
HEUTE BASTELN WIR
EINE LAMPE

BUY
① 📏 2× PAPER & CUT IT IN 6 STRIPES

70

100

✂

② SCOTCH (TESA)

1/3 1/3 1/3

③ FOLD IT LIKE AN ACCORDEON
(FALTE ES WIE EIN...)

④ LOCH EISEN (CATEUR)

MAKE A HOLE
(MACH EIN LOCH)

13,5   5

SO CUTE!
SÜSS!

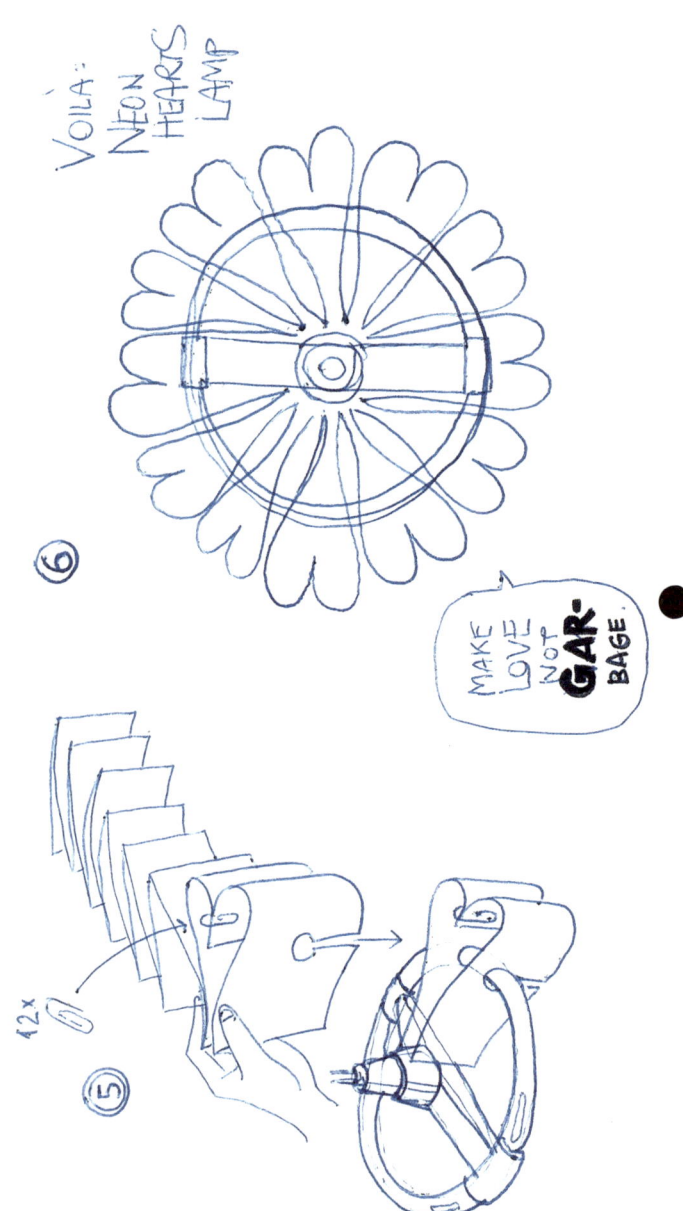

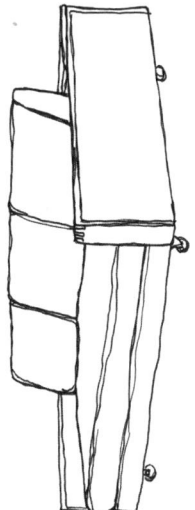

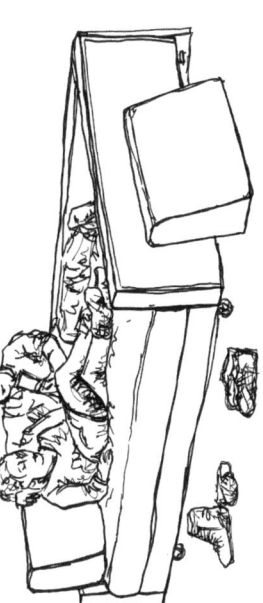

Daytime: **Sofa for loungers** /
Am Tag: Sofa für Rumlümmler
Nighttime: Bed for lovers /
Nachts: Bett für Liebende

si
wo
sofa

350 € (+ mattress / Matratze)

3.5 days / 3,5 Tage

Difficulty level / Schwierigkeitsgrad **++**

W x D x H / B x T x H: **220 x 146 x 70 cm**

Illustration (on this spread / auf dieser

Doppelseite): **Sabine Schmidt**

Inspiration

Daybed
1950s / 1950er-Jahre
Hans J. Wegner

Lounge Collection
1954
Florence Knoll

SHOPPING-LIST (CM)

- KIEFER LEIMHOLZ (38 MM!)
  L (B)
  - 2x (146) x (16) (B1 . B2)

- KIEFER LEIMHOLZ (28 MM !)
  L   B
  - 2x (200) x (14)   (B3, B4)
  - 2x (200) x (10)   (B5)
  - 1x (200) x (24)   (B8)
  - 2x (146) x (10)   (A1, A2)
  - 4x (41) x (10)   (A3, A4, A5, A6)

- KIEFER LEIMHOLZ (18 MM)
  L   (B)
  - 1x 220 x 50   (C1)

- SPERRHOLZ   (12 MM)
  L   B
  - 2x 139 x 37,5   (A7, A8)
  - 2x 139 x 26,5   (A9, A10)

- KIEFER - RECHTECK LEISTEN (MM)
  - 2x [////] L = 140cm (A11, A12)
      9   20
  - 2x [////] L = 200cm (C2, C3)
      9   20
  - 4x [////] L = 24cm (A13, A14, A15, A16)
      9   20
  - 2x [==] L = 185cm (B6, B7)
      8   20

- 1x FÖRSTNER BOHRER Ø 35MM

- 4x SCHREIBTISCH-PLATTENVERBINDER Ø 35MM
  ↔ 65MM

- [6cm] · 4x ROLLEN

- DÜBEL
  - 9x Ø 12MM
  - 16x Ø 6MM

You can build parts:
A, B and C.
The rest please buy.
(MATRESS, LATTENROST,
POLSTER ...)

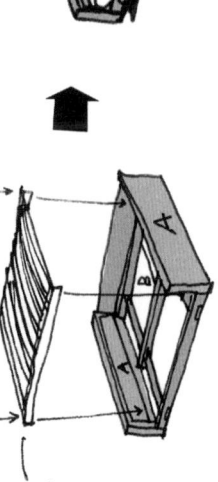

POLSTERX
13 [ ] 37
↔ 66
20

MATRESS
140 x 200
H = 11 - 14 "?"

IKEA
20,€

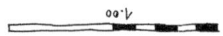

1.00

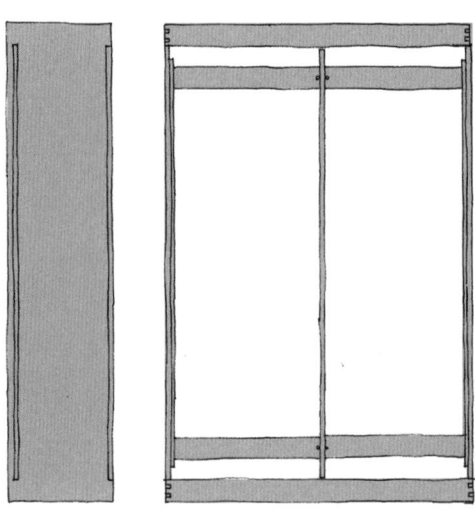

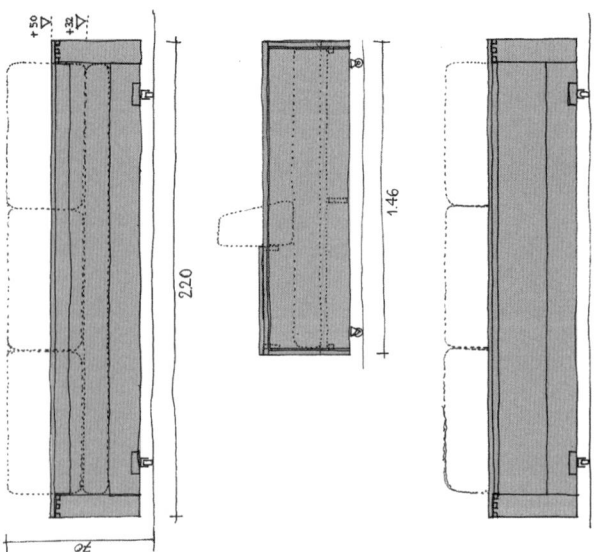

220

1.46

+ 50

+ 32

70

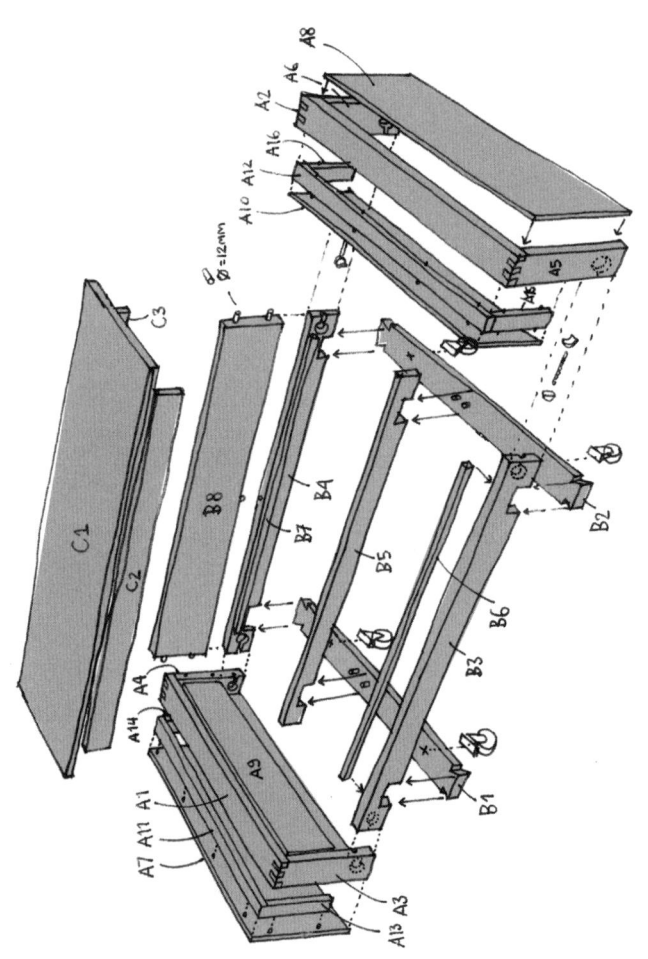

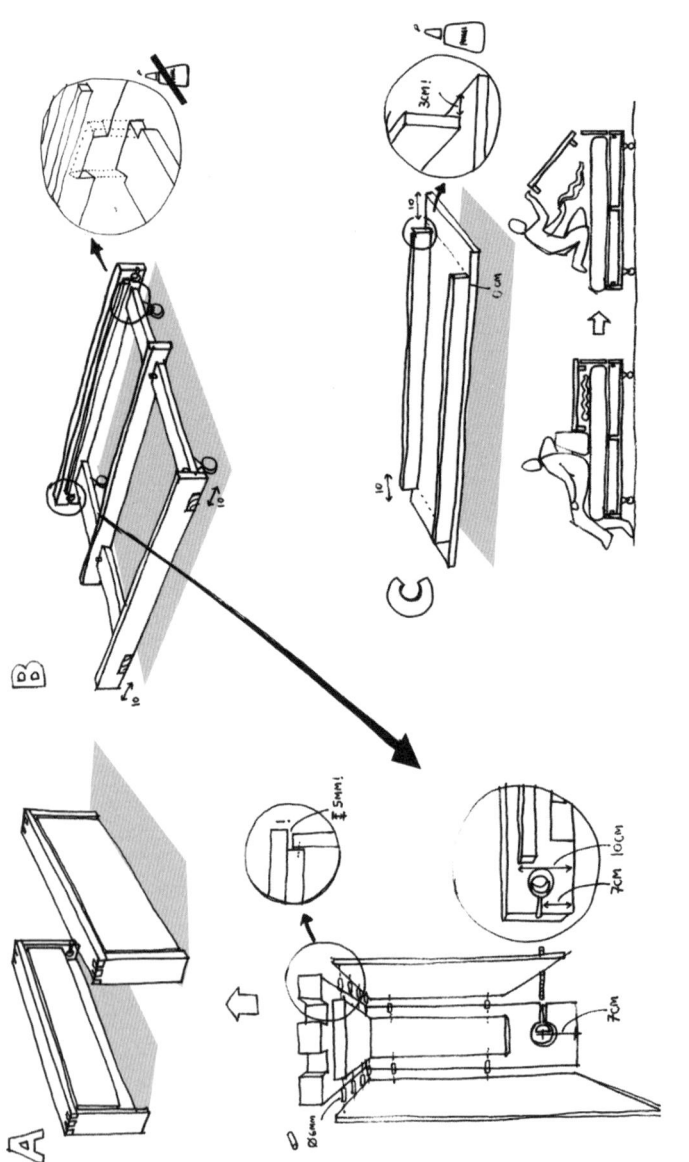

A

B

C

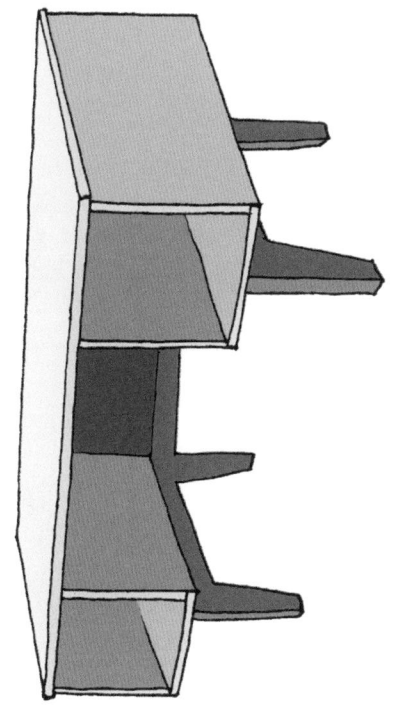

neu
koelln
desk

150 €

15 hours / Stunden

Difficu ty level / Schwierigkeitsgrad ++

W x D x H / B x T x H: 150 x 80 x 68 cm

Illustration (on this spread / auf dieser

Doppelseite): **Tammo Winkler**

Inspiration

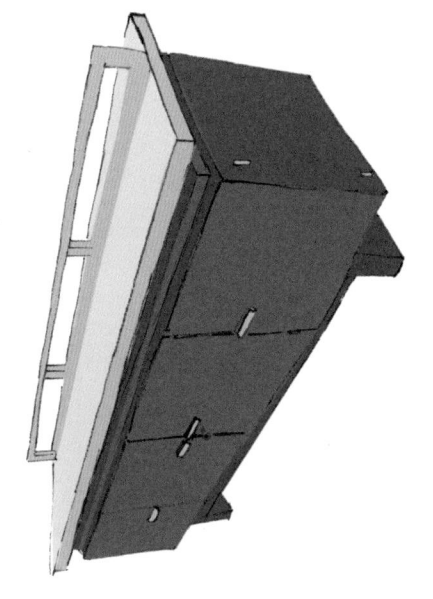

New York Sideboard
1928
Bruno Paul

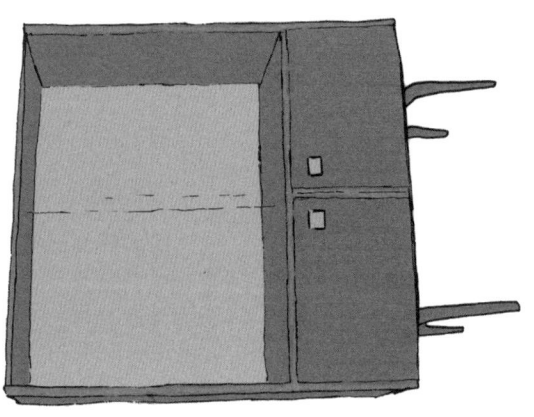

T-Serie
1964
Franz Ehrlich

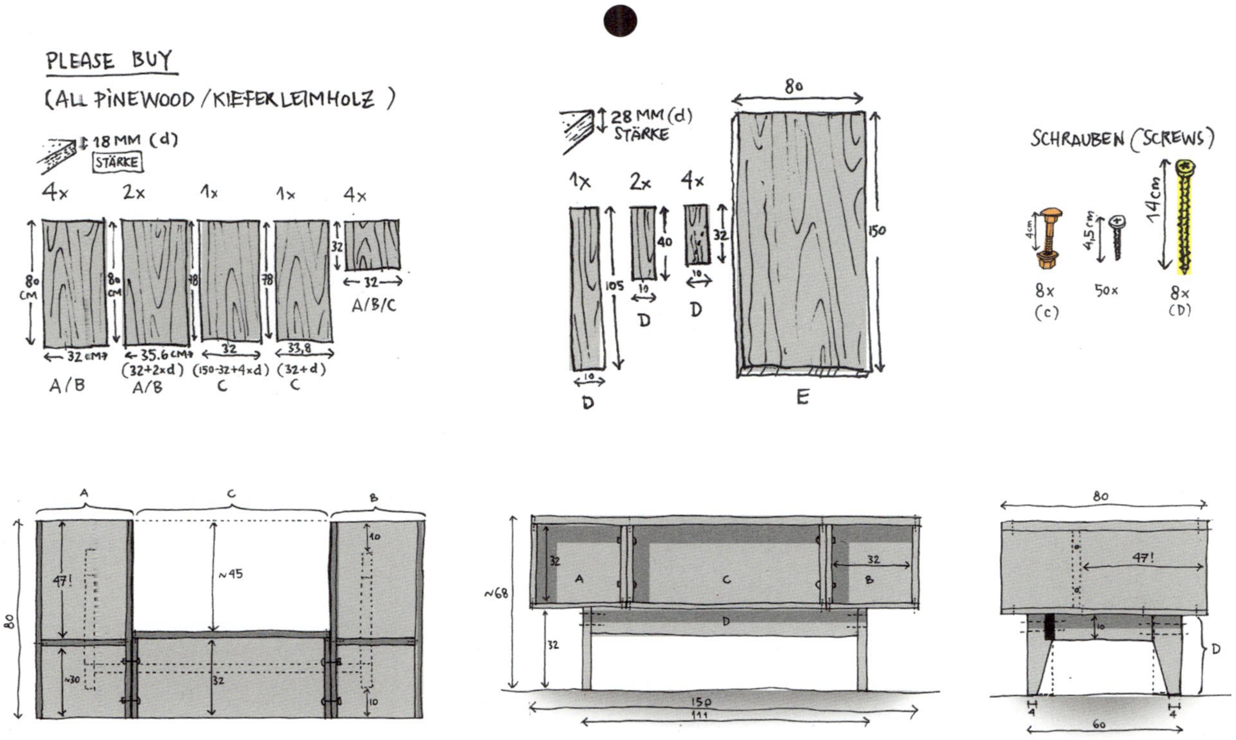

PLEASE BUY
(ALL PINEWOOD / KIEFERLEIMHOLZ)
18 MM (d) STÄRKE
4x
2x
1x
1x
4x
80 CM
80 CM
78
78
32
32 CM
35.6 CM
(32+2xd)
32
(150-32+4xd)
33,8
(32+d)
32
A/B
A/B
C
C
A/B/C
28 MM (d) STÄRKE
1x
2x
4x
105
10
D
40
10
D
32
10
D
80
150
E
SCHRAUBEN (SCREWS)
4cm
8x
(C)
4,5cm
50x
14cm
8x
(D)
A
C
B
80
47!
~30
~45
32
10
10
~68
32
A
C
B
D
32
32
150
111
80
47!
10
D
4
4
60

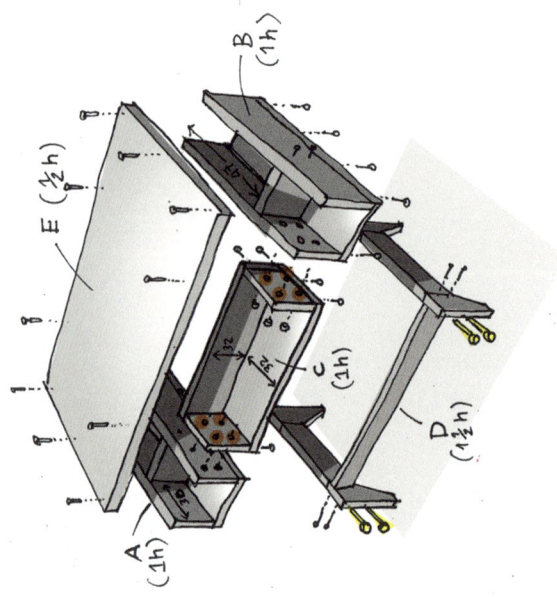

A
(1h)

B
(1h)

C
(1h)

D
(1½h)

E
(½h)

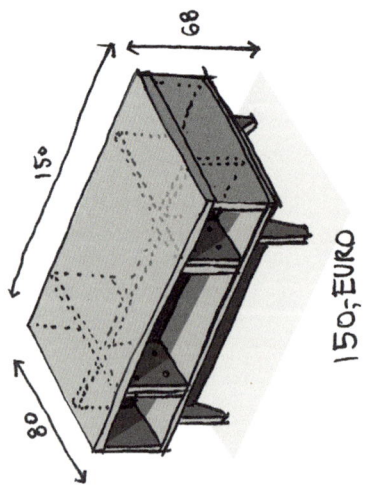

68

15°

80

150,-EURO

Space for your design /
Freiraum für Deinen Entwurf:

Pigeon blue / Taubenblau –
approx. / etwa RAL 5014

Perfect for walls and tabletops (Piscator Table) / Perfekt für
Wände und Tischplatten (Piscator Table)

com m unity

A World on the Basis
of Give-and-Take

Eine Welt bestehend aus
Geben und Nehmen

●

Texts / Texte: Birgit S. Bauer, Kristin Hensel,
Rebecca Sandbichler, Marie Voigt, Mathias Wetzl
Photos / Fotos: Katrin Brunner, Peter Empl,
Osman Erdogan, Emrullah Gümüşsoy, Nadine
Krüger, Judith Langner, Ib Voss Pedersen, Hartmut
Raiser, Janina Schuster, Michaela Siegel, Robert
J. Swartz, Jan Vailhé, Linnéa Weitkamp, Robert
Ziegler, Vittorio Zincone

What would the Hartz-IV project be without the Community? It wouldn't be a project at all. Only a website that offers building plans for download. Build more, buy less! Only the enthusiasm of the national and international Community has filled the building plans with life. Quite individual interpretations and even further developments in design have emerged and filled every single builder with great pride. Here you can learn who these people are and what stories they have to tell you.

Marie Voigt

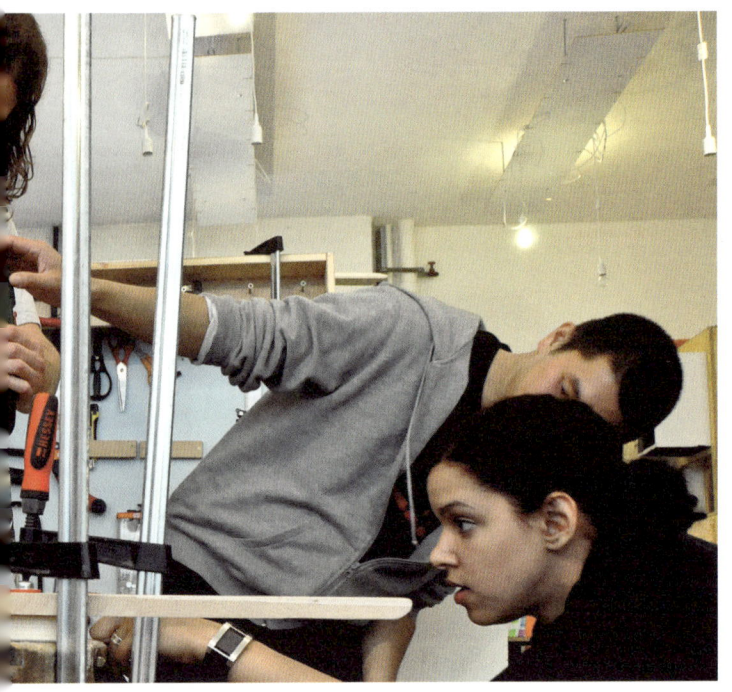

Was wäre das Hartz-IV-Projekt ohne die Community? Es wäre gar kein Projekt. Nur eine Webseite, die Baupläne zum Download anbietet. Konstruieren statt konsumieren! Einzig und allein die Begeisterung der internationalen Community flößte den Bauplänen Leben ein. Es entstanden ganz eigene Interpretationen und auch Weiterentwicklungen der Designstücke, und sie erfüllten jeden einzelnen Erbauer mit großem Stolz. Hier erfahrt Ihr, wer diese Menschen sind und welche Geschichte sie Euch zu erzählen haben.

Marie Voigt

Nele Ouwens, Berlin, Germany
Kreuzberg-36-Chair

Nele came to building furniture rather accidentally: her friend Mona had signed up for a workshop but was unable to attend. So Nele went. "I was new in Berlin and it was a great opportunity to get to know people and do something creative." Although the thirty-one-year-old graphic artist and painter enjoys working with her hands, she doesn't have much experience with handicrafts. "It's difficult to achieve the precision that you need so that everything is perfect," Nele finds. That's why she isn't really 100 percent satisfied with her Kreuzberg-36-Chair. "A second one would surely be even better ..." Mona, however, seems to like Nele's chair. It stands next to her kitchen table.

Nele kam eher zufällig zum Möbelbauen: Ihre Freundin Mona hatte einen Workshop gebucht und konnte nicht hingehen. Also ging eben Nele. »Ich war neu in Berlin, und es war eine super Möglichkeit, Leute kennenzulernen und etwas Kreatives zu machen.« Die 31-jährige Grafikerin und Malerin arbeitet gerne mit den Händen, ist aber handwerklich nicht so geübt. »Die Präzision, die man braucht, damit alles perfekt wird, ist schwer zu erreichen«, findet Nele. Darum ist sie mit ihrem Kreuzberg-36-Chair auch nicht hundertprozentig zufrieden. »Ein zweiter würde sicher noch besser werden …« Mona scheint Neles Stuhl aber zu gefallen. Er steht an ihrem Küchentisch.

Johannes Schreiter, Cologne, Germany

24-Euro-Chair, Berliner Hocker

There is a first time for everything, even for Johannes Schreiter, who was the first person in the world to recreate the 24-Euro-Chair—eagerly, but haunted by bad luck. The hardware store cut the wood incorrectly so that the chair turned out ten centimeters wider. For cost reasons, the trained social pedagogue chose soft spruce wood instead of pine. And since he didn't have clamps on hand, he used tape instead without further ado, and then fixed everything with umpteen screws. He built the 24-Euro-Chair in just a few hours, bravo! Sadly, it didn't hold up! It was the one-hundred-kilo weight of a friend that finally made the first work collapse. But this impassioned builder, who runs an online shop (www.noe-shop.de), learns from mistakes: his coffee table consisting of four Berliner Hocker is still standing and looks just great in his apartment!

Alles macht man zum ersten Mal, auch Johannes Schreiter, der eifrig, aber vom Pech verfolgt, den 24-Euro-Chair als weltweit Erster nachbaute. Im Baumarkt wurde falsch zugeschnitten, sodass der Stuhl zehn Zentimeter breiter wurde. Aus Kostengründen wählte der gelernte Sozialpädagoge weiches Fichtenholz statt Kiefer. Und da keine Zwingen zur Hand waren, wurde kurzerhand Klebeband zum Pressen benutzt. Alles noch mit zig Schrauben fixiert. Den 24-Euro-Chair hat er in wenigen Stunden gebaut, bravo! Nur gehalten hat er nicht! Spätestens das 100-Kilo-Gewicht eines Freundes brachte das Erstlingswerk zum Einsturz. Doch aus Fehlern hat der bauwütige Betreiber eines Onlineshops (www.noe-shop.de) gelernt, sein Couchtisch aus vier Berliner Hockern hält Stand und sieht dazu noch toll in der Wohnung aus!

Geert Vullings, Ottersum, Netherlands
24-Euro-Chair

Excerpt from an e-mail of March 5, 2012: "I am not an interesting person. (77 years old and in the clutches of mister Parkinson.) Only a man who still tries to hold his head up, and who finds it difficult to participate in a real conversation. But I made the chair and am happy with the result. I found the idea and the design of Le Van Bo very beautiful. I still owe him a photo of the chair. I wish him and you good luck. Geert Vullings."

Dear Geert, we wish you the same!

Van Bo Le-Mentzel and the Crowd

Auszug aus einer Mail vom 5. März 2012: »Ich bin kein interessanter Menschen. (77 jahren alt und in dem Griff von mister Parkinson.) Nur ein Mann der noch versucht aufrecht zu gehen und der fast nicht mehr an eine richtige Konversation teilnehmen kann. Ich habe den Stuhl aber fertig gestelt und bin zufrieden mit das Resultat. Ich fand die Idee un das Entwurf von Le Van Bo sehr schön. Ich bin ihm noch ein foto von den Stuhl schuldig. Ich wünche Ihm und Ihnen viel Glück. Geert Vullings.«

Lieber Geert, das wünschen wir Dir auch.

Van Bo Le-Mentzel und die Crowd

Pieter van der Kooij,
Rotterdam,
Netherlands
Berliner Hocker

Björn Urnauer,
Frankfurt am Main, Germany
Kreuzberg-36-Chair

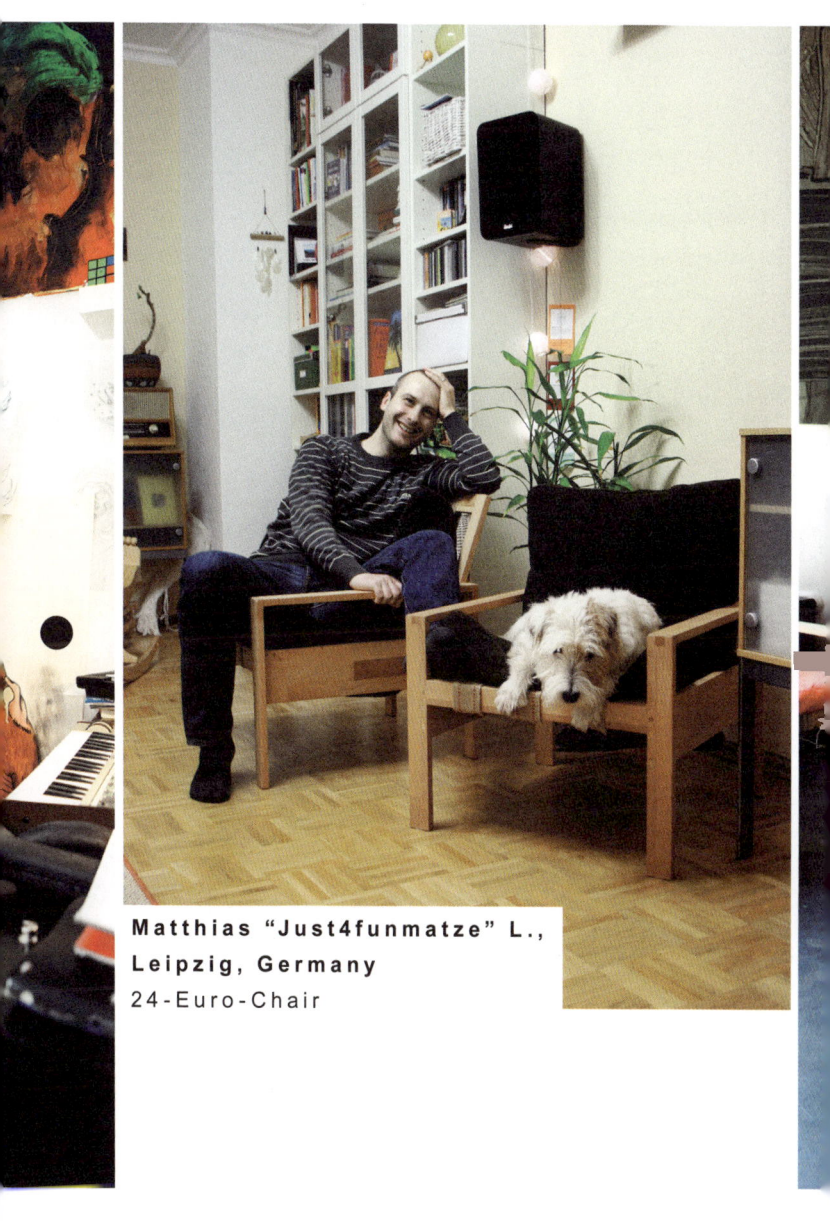

Matthias "Just4funmatze" L.,
Leipzig, Germany
24-Euro-Chair

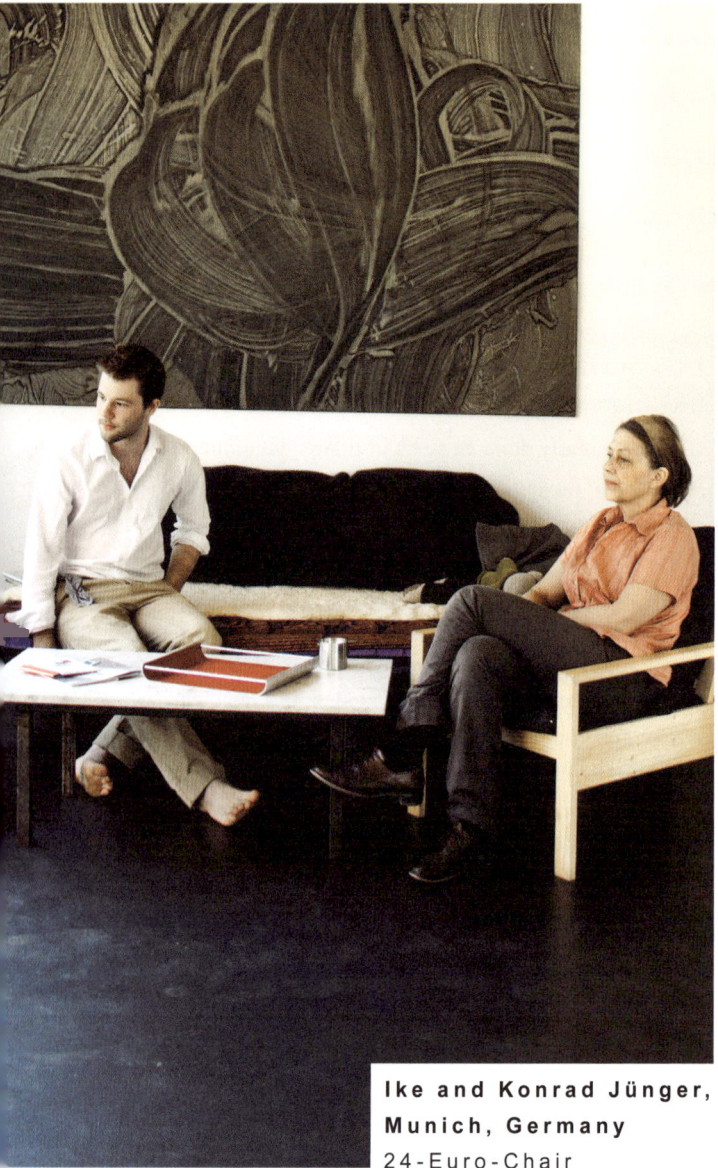

**Ike and Konrad Jünger,
Munich, Germany**
24-Euro-Chair

Dirk Harms, Hannover, Germany
Berliner Hocker, Radio Hartz-IV-Empfänger

Dirk has already done all sorts of things, including working as a soundproofing engineer, a building energy consultant, and an office manager. Although it sounds interesting, it was also damned strenuous. When the carousel started turning at an increasingly higher speed at some point, he jumped off and decided to "dedicate himself to art and develop speakers." In this phase he read about Van Bo Le-Mentzel and his Hartz-IV-Möbel. "I thought the idea was great," says Dirk. But he also had his own idea: speakers for everybody—complete with amplifiers. Van Bo then named it the "Hartz-IV-Empfänger" (German welfare receiver, a play on the expression German welfare recipient). Inspired by the Berliner Hocker and the Braun radios of the nineteen-sixties, Dirk developed a device, radio, and docking station in one, which is technically sophisticated and a real beauty yet possible to build oneself. Says Dirk: "Housing about 45 minutes with all the drill holes, electronics about 2 hours." Nonetheless, the Hartz-IV-Empfänger should accompany its owner for a lifetime. Dirk has a lot of plans for the future. He would like to develop other speakers, organize a sculpture exhibition, establish himself as an artist, support other artists, and write books—but everything without any pressure. Although Dirk is already busy again, this time everything seems to be right.

Dirk war schon alles Mögliche, unter anderem Schallschutzingenieur, Gebäudeenergieberater und Büroleiter. Klingt interessant, aber als sich das Karussell irgendwann immer schneller drehte, sprang er ab und beschloss, sich »der Kunst zu widmen und Lautsprecher zu entwickeln«. Er las von Van Bo Le-Mentzel und seinen Hartz-IV-Möbeln. »Ich fand seine Ideen großartig«, sagt Dirk. Er hatte aber auch eigene: Lautsprecher für alle, komplett mit Verstärker. Van Bo nannte das dann Hartz-IV-Empfänger. Inspiriert vom Berliner Hocker und den Braun-Radios der 1960er-Jahre entwickelte Dirk ein Gerät, Radio und Dockingstation in einem, das dennoch selbst gebaut werden kann. Dirk: »Gehäuse etwa 45 Minuten mit allen Bohrungen, Elektronik etwa 2 Stunden.« Trotzdem soll der Hartz-IV-Empfänger seinen Besitzer ein Leben lang begleiten. In Zukunft möchte Dirk weiter Lautsprecher entwickeln, eine Skulpturenausstellung aufbauen, sich als Künstler etablieren, andere Künstler fördern und Bücher schreiben. Aber alles ohne Druck. Dirk macht schon wieder eine Menge, aber diesmal scheint alles zu stimmen.

Ole Kloss, Berlin, Germany
Kreuzberg-36-Chair with recycled paper

An old architect and designer saying: form follows function. When the form is already there, the suitable function just has to be found. And so Ole realized: the rounding at the end of the human spine fits perfectly into the parts of an advertising pillar that had already been lying around his apartment for a while. Its frame then led to the building plan for the Kreuzberg-36-Chair. Unfortunately, after the chair was built, it became clear that the backrest had turned out to be quite steep. The consequence: one has to sit very straight. Function also sometimes follows form ...

Alte Architekten- und Designerweisheit: Form folgt Funktion. Wenn die Form schon da ist, muss man sich eben
die passende Funktion suchen. Und so stellte Ole fest:
Die Rundung am Ende des menschlichen Rückens
passt perfekt in die Teile einer Litfasssäule, die schon
eine Weile bei ihm herumlagen. Das Gerüst dazu lieferte
dann der Bauplan für den Kreuzberg-36-Chair. Leider
stellte sich nach dem Bau heraus, dass die Rücken-
Lehne ziemlich steil geworden war. Die Folge: Man muss
sehr gerade sitzen. Funktion folgt eben manchmal auch
Form ...

Kristin Hensel, Berlin, Germany
Berliner Hocker, 24-Euro-Chair

"In den Adern des Holzes seh ich Gesichter" (I see faces in the grain of wood). These lyrics from the German band Tocotronic might also have come from Kristin. The Berlin fashion designer has brought wood and fabric together in many designs, including in the upholstery cover for the 24-Euro-Chair. Although she had already built the furniture for her shop herself, this project was very special to her: "Working together in the workshop, the smell of wood and glue, it was just wonderful."

»In den Adern des Holzes seh ich Gesichter.« Die Lied-
zeile der deutschen Band Tocotronic könnte auch von
Kristin sein. Die Berliner Modedesignerin hat schon in
vielen Entwürfen Holz und Stoff vereint, auch im Polster-
bezug für den 24-Euro-Chair. Obwohl sie schon ihre
Shopeinrichtung selbst gebaut hat, war dieses Projekt
für sie ganz besonders: »Das gemeinsame Arbeiten in
der Werkstatt, der Geruch von Holz und Leim, das war
wundervoll.«

Marie Voigt, Berlin, Germany
24-Euro-Chair, Beta Block, Berliner
Hocker

Marie needs a thirty-two-hour day. As employer brand manager, she passionately works all over Germany for her company, Deutsche Bahn. She would also like to write a doctoral thesis and enjoy the vibrant life of Berlin as often as possible. And then there's another wonderful time-consuming activity: the wardrobe that she is currently building from old doors and windows. Thank goodness she doesn't have a house yet—since she wants to build the house herself, along with all the furniture inside. For the time being, she builds pieces of furniture at her mother's house and stores them there. Her next projects are of course already waiting to be realized. Hopefully, a thirty-two-hour day will then still be enough ...

Marie braucht den 32-Stunden-Tag. Für ihren Arbeitgeber, die Deutsche Bahn, ist sie bundesweit als Employer Brand Managerin im Einsatz. Dann möchte sie auch noch eine Doktorarbeit schreiben und so oft es geht das vibrierende Berliner Leben genießen. Und dann ist da noch dieser wunderschöne Zeitfresser: Ein Kleiderschrank aus alten Türen und Fenstern, den sie gerade baut. Gott sei Dank hat sie noch kein Haus – denn dieses und die darin stehenden Möbel sollen einmal alle selbst gemacht sein. Bis es soweit ist, werden die Möbelstücke bei Mutti zu Hause gebaut und geparkt. Die nächsten Projekte sind natürlich schon in Arbeit. Hoffentlich reicht ihr dann der 32-Stunden-Tag noch aus …

Sandra Ae-Sim Schleicher,
Berlin, Germany
Kreuzberg-36-Chair

Batiste Pascalin, Teltow, Germany
Kreuzberg-36-Chair

Batiste made it. To fulfill his passion, he created his own workshop in his house—tinkering with old Vespas and motorbikes. Since he used to spend more time working with metal, he really appreciated the simplicity of wood as a material. His scrapbook is full of ideas because he would really like to do much more designing. Favorite saying? "The one who always does what he already can do, will always be what he already is." (Henry Ford)

Batiste hat es geschafft. Er hat sich für seine Leidenschaft – an alten Vespas und Motorrädern schrauben – eine eigene Werkstatt in seinem Haus geschaffen. Da er in der Vergangenheit mehr mit Metall gearbeitet hat, weiß er die Einfachheit von Holz als Werkstoff sehr zu schätzen. Entwerfen möchte er gern noch mehr. Das Scrapbook mit Ideen hat er schon. Lieblingszitat? »Wer immer tut, was er schon kann, wird immer bleiben, was er ist.« (Henry Ford)

Nico Beyer, Berlin, Germany
Beta Block, Berliner Hocker
www.beyer-soehne.de

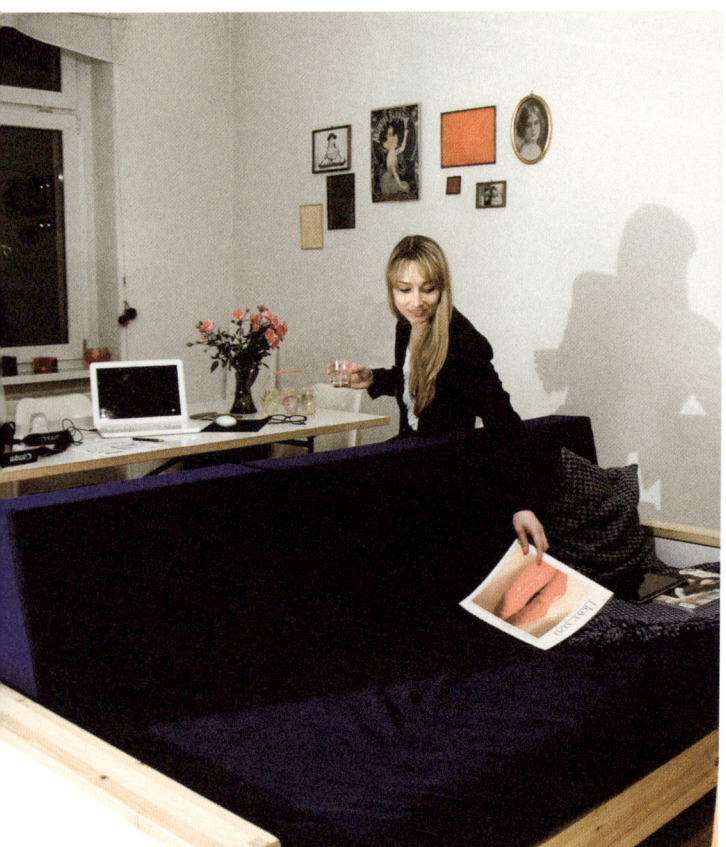

Anke Buchmann, Berlin, Germany
SiWo-Sofa

**Jesko Bendmann,
Hamburg, Germany**
Berliner Hocker

**Georg Witoszynskyj,
Vienna, Austria**
100-Sec-Lamp

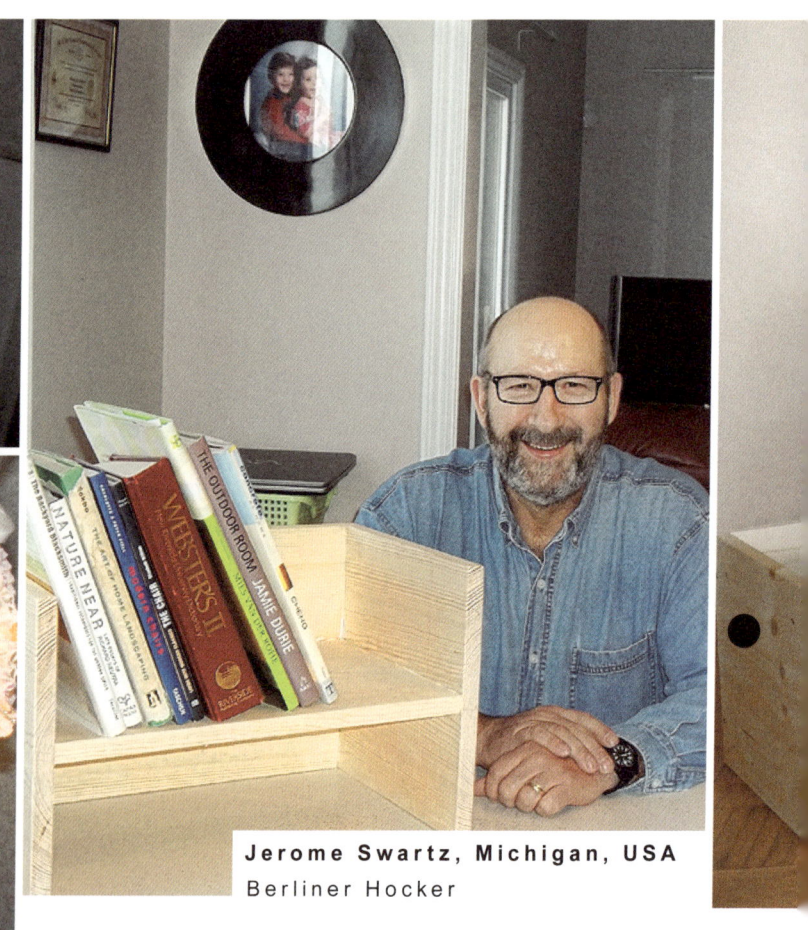

Jerome Swartz, Michigan, USA
Berliner Hocker

Judith Langner,
Bavarian Forest, Germany
Berliner Hocker as children's kitchen

Joachim E. Weitkamp,
Bielefeld, Germany
Kreuzberg-36-Chair (mini version)

Hartmut Raiser, Stuttgart, Germany
24-Euro-Chair, Berliner Hocker

"Less is more," said Ludwig Mies van der Rohe, who would have taken pleasure in the colorful furnishings of the café at the Treiber Bakery in Bernhausen near Stuttgart. Here they are: the armchairs, stools, and benches from the range of Hartz-IV-Möbel. Planned and realized by Hartmut Raiser, a professor of interior design from Darmstadt, and built by two of his students from Kazakhstan. Though they are all professionals, they nonetheless very much enjoyed building the furniture.

»Weniger ist mehr«, sagte Ludwig Mies van der Rohe und hätte seine Freude an der bunten Ausstattung des Bäckereicafés Treiber in Bernhausen bei Stuttgart gehabt. Hier stehen sie, die Sessel, Hocker und Bänke aus dem Hartz-IV-Möbel-Programm. Geplant und umgesetzt von Innenarchitektur-Professor Hartmut Raiser aus Darmstadt und von zwei seiner Studenten aus Kasachstan geschreinert. Die sind zwar alle Profis, hatten aber dennoch viel Freude beim Bauen.

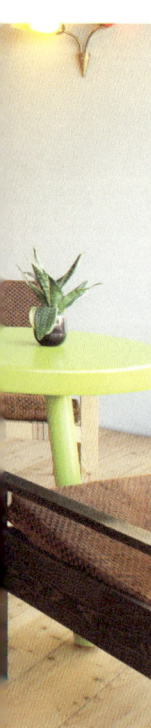

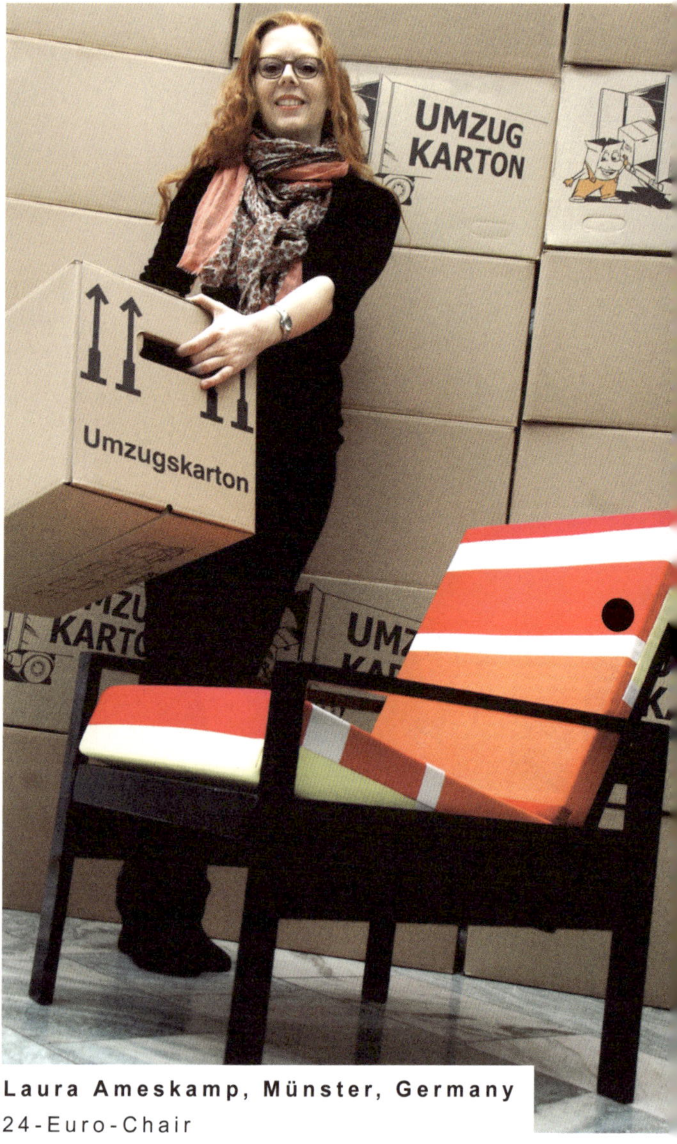

Laura Ameskamp, Münster, Germany
24-Euro-Chair

Fehmi Hoffmann, Berlin, Germany
Piscator Table, Kreuzberg-36-Chair

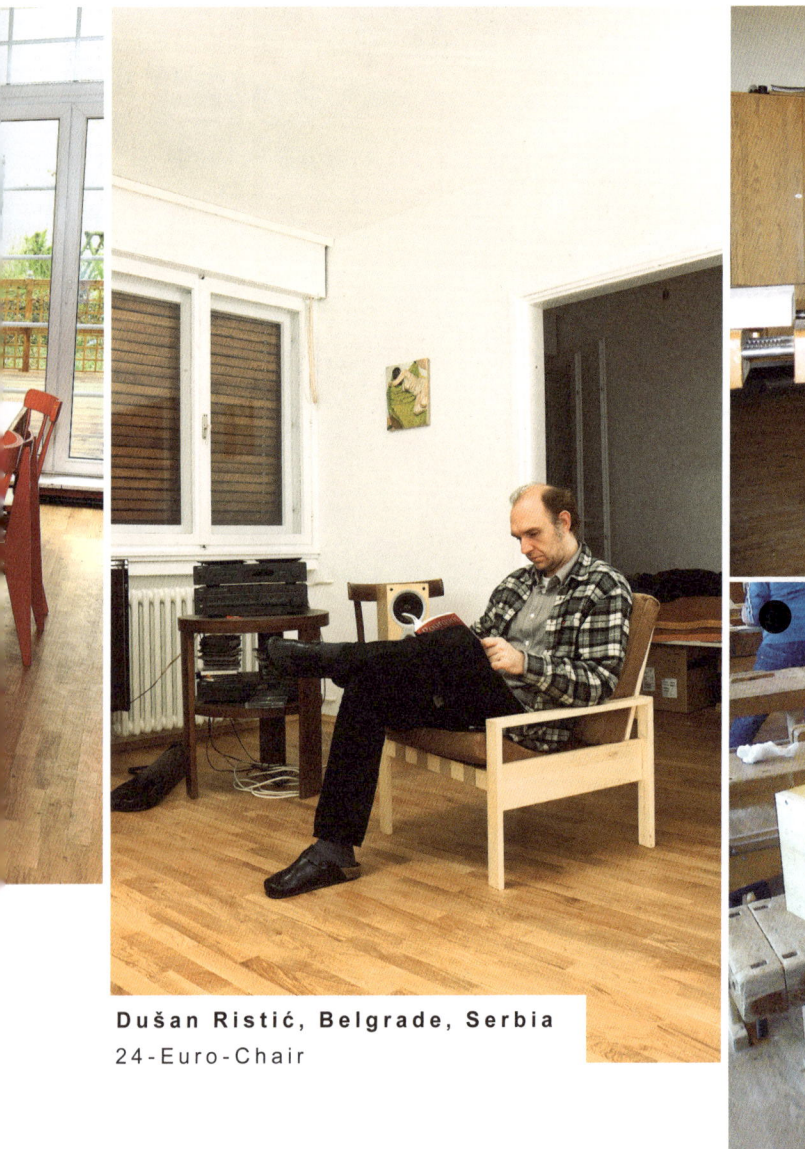

Dušan Ristić, Belgrade, Serbia
24-Euro-Chair

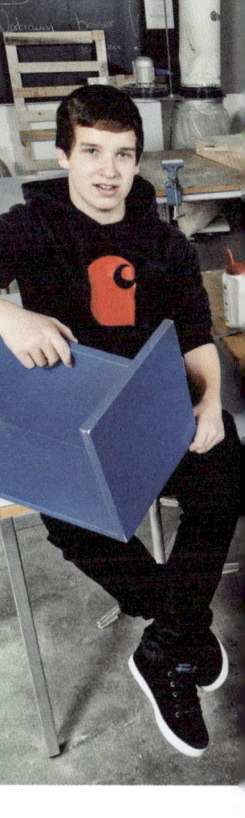

Morton W. Perdersen,
Horsens, Denmark
Berliner Hocker, 24-Euro-Chair

**Thomas Arbenz,
Matzendorf, Switzerland**
Berliner Hocker,
Kreuzberg-36-Chair

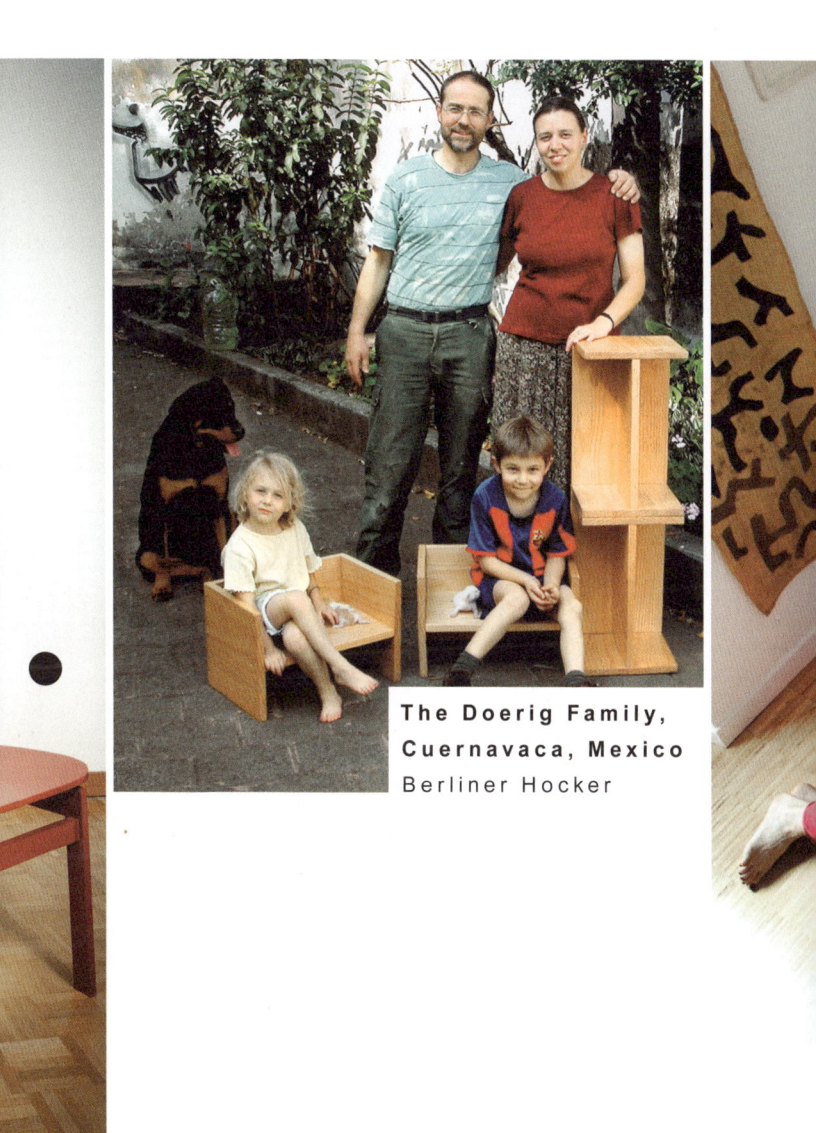

**The Doerig Family,
Cuernavaca, Mexico**
Berliner Hocker

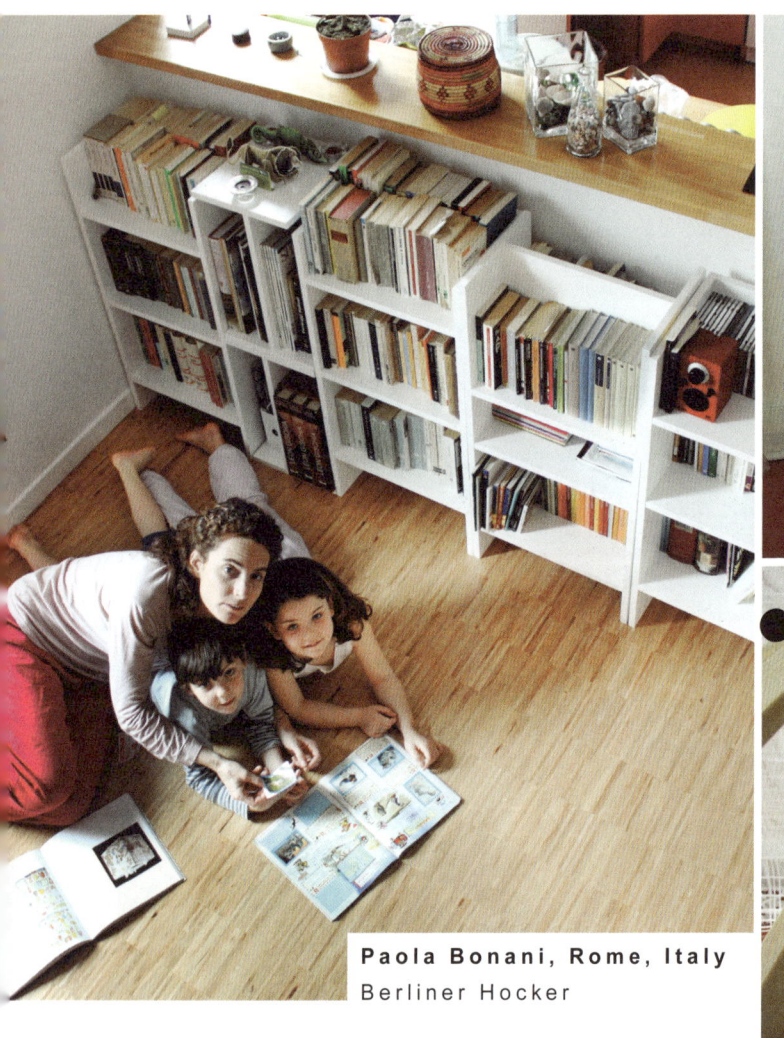

Paola Bonani, Rome, Italy
Berliner Hocker

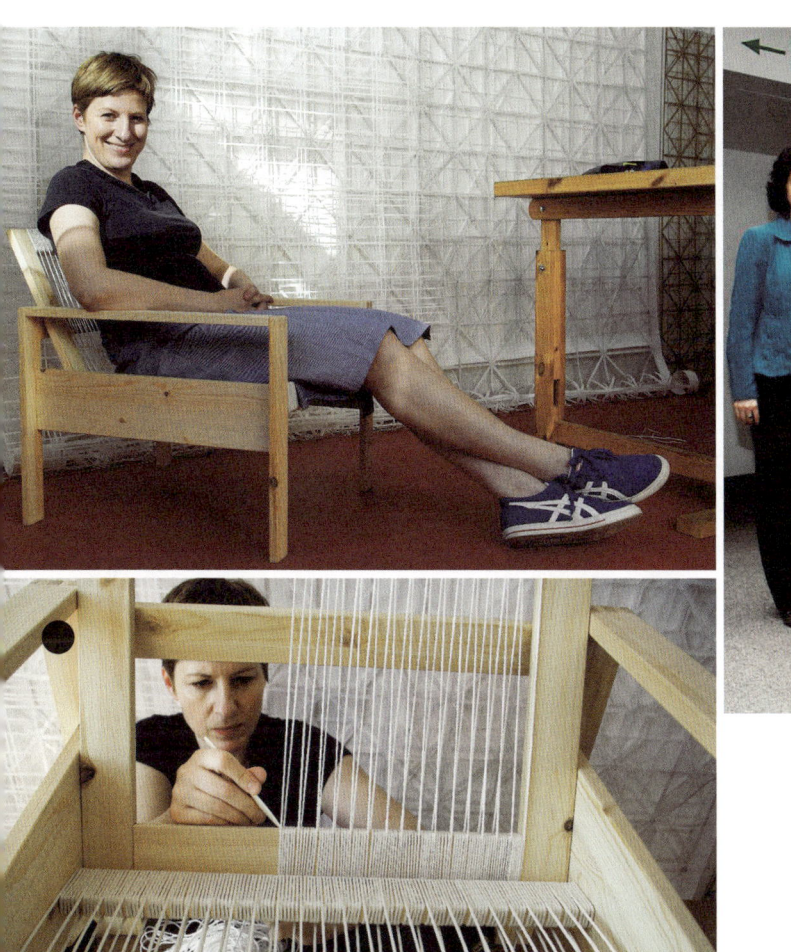

Stefka Ammon, Berlin, Germany
24-Euro-Chair

Manfred Stoffl, Montreal, Canada
Kreuzberg-36-Chair

The team of the Goethe-Institut in Montréal is so happy! Under the supervision of Manfred Stoffl, the director of the institute, three Kreuzberg-36-Chairs were created in three days. The chairs, which are situated right at the entrance to the institute, are now welcoming visitors. "Painting them in the institute's colors was the easiest part of the building process," the greenhorns in woodworking mentioned. The Canadians had imagined that everything else would have been easier, but they stuck to their motto: "We can do it!" Now, only the sofa is missing.

Stolz wie Oskar ist das Team des Goethe-Instituts Montreal auf die drei Kreuzberg-36-Chairs, die in drei Tagen unter dem Leiter des Instituts, Manfred Stoffl, entstanden. Gleich am Eingang kann man sich jetzt auf die in Institutsfarben gestrichenen Stühle setzen – der Anstrich war dann auch das Einfachste am Bau der Stühle, sagen die Holzbau-Greenhorns. Alles andere hatten sich die Kanadier einfacher vorgestellt, blieben aber bei ihrem Motto: »Das machen wir!« Jetzt fehlt nur noch das Sofa.

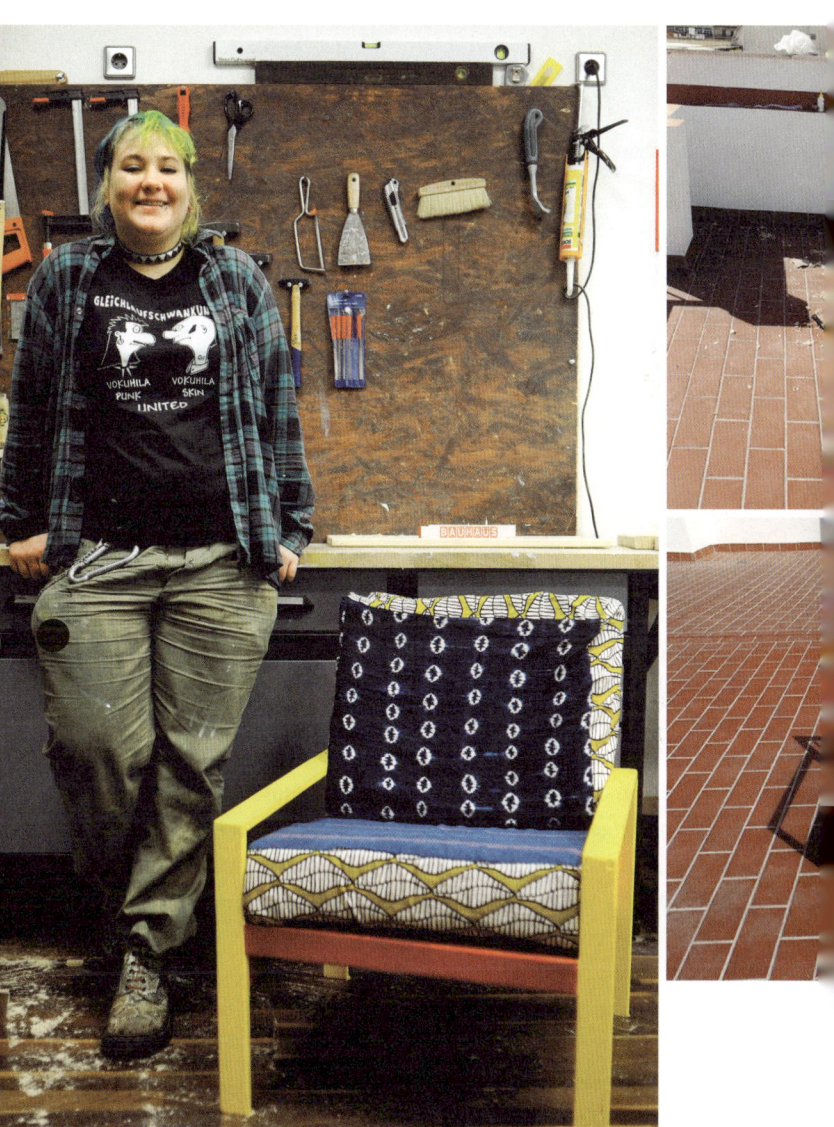

Pia Waschko, Karlsruhe, Germany
24-Euro-Chair

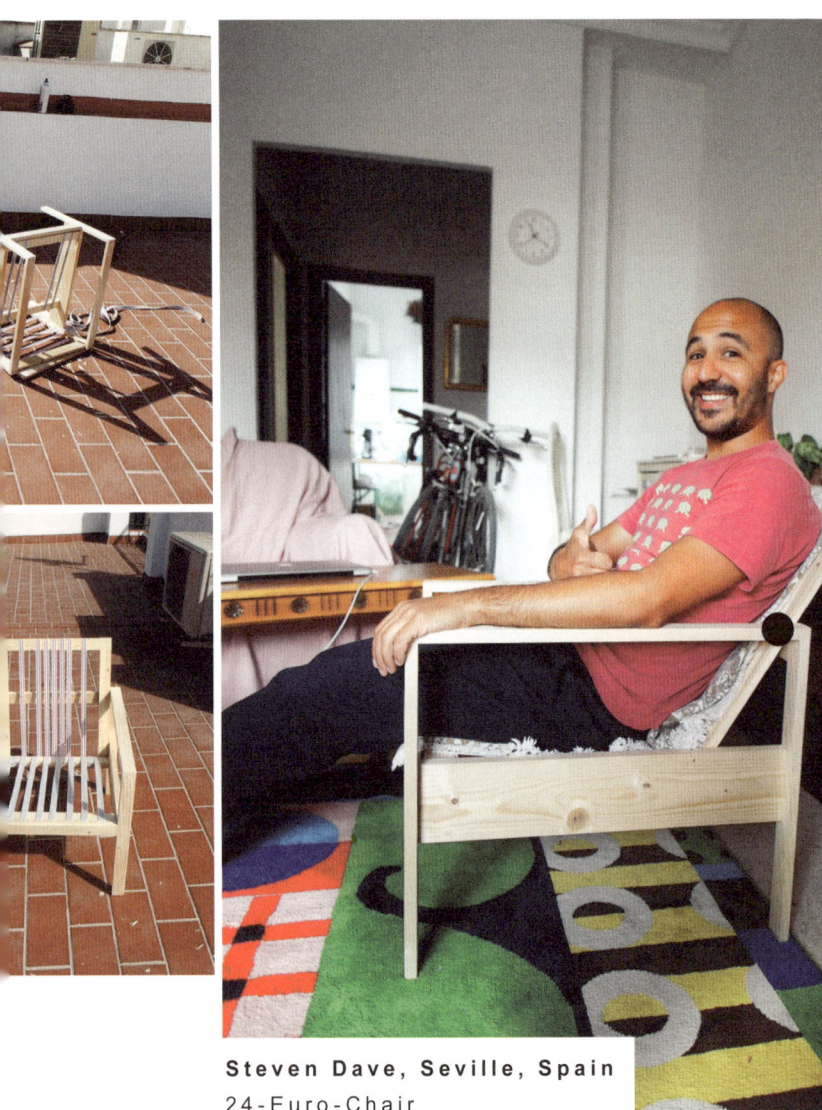

Steven Dave, Seville, Spain
24-Euro-Chair

Space for your story /
Freiraum für Deine Geschichte:

Flame red / Feuerrot –
approx. / etwa RAL 3000

Perfect for the Kreuzberg-36-Chair / Perfekt für den
Kreuzberg-36-Chair

karma
eco
nomy

**The Power of Giving
and Taking**

Die Kraft des Gebens
und Nehmens

Text: **Van Bo Le-Mentzel**
Collaboration / Mitarbeit: **the Crowd,
in particular** / die Crowd, besonders **Regine Lin,
Julia Meyer, Stanislav Bugaev, Simon Wind,
Marie Voigt, and** / und **Danny Iny**

Take Care of Your Karma

My friends were a bit taken aback when they saw my mother. She had shaved off her hair and was wearing a robe. "From now on, I am no longer only there for you, my son, but for all children," she said. It was her way of dealing with the sadness that had been triggered by the death of her father in Pakse, the only remaining member of our family in Laos. She began a new life in a Buddhist monastery. As a nun with the name Co Hanh Nhu—the bright mother—she was happy once again. I was fourteen. That was the day I lost my mother—and gained a new perspective. I visited her in the monastery every year. She told me a lot about her motivation, about why people plod along eternally in the hamster wheel, and about letting go. We sat on the waxed wooden floor of the prayer hall and spoke about happiness and suffering. She believed that as long as I did good deeds, I would be charging my Karma. She herself had her difficulties letting go. Throughout her life she had pursued one dream: building a small Buddhist monastery in Berlin. At that time, there was not yet a Facebook and no crowd funding. But she succeeded, nevertheless, in gathering a large crowd and had soon collected 10,000 euros. How did she do it? I learned a lot from her. Basically, it's very easy: take care that your life is balanced between giving and taking, and you will find happiness. Take care of your Karma.

Exchange Openness for Building Plans

Twenty years later, I made a name for myself with Hartz-IV-Möbel project. I do not sell the building plans. I give them away. Well, that's not entirely true. I do expect something in return: a story. People pay me with openness. Giving and taking. Charging my

Achte auf
Dein Karma

Meine Freunde staunten nicht schlecht, als sie meine Mutter sahen. Sie hatte sich die Haare abrasiert und trug ein Gewand. »Ab jetzt bin ich nicht mehr nur für Dich da, mein Sohn, sondern für alle Kinder«, sagte sie. Es war ihr Weg aus der Trauer, der durch den Tod ihres Vaters in Pakse ausgelöst wurde. Der einzige Hinterbliebene unserer Familie in Laos. Sie begann ein neues Leben in einem buddhistischen Kloster. Als Nonne mit dem Namen Co Hanh Nhu – die lichte Mutter – wurde sie wieder glücklich. Ich war vierzehn. Das war der Tag, an dem ich meine Mutter verlor – und eine neue Perspektive gewann. Ich besuchte sie jedes Jahr im Kloster. Sie erzählte mir viel über Motivation. Darüber, warum Menschen sich ewig im Hamsterrad abmühen. Und über das Loslassen. Wir saßen auf dem gebohnerten Holzboden des Gebetsaals und sprachen über Glück und Leid. Sie meinte, solange ich Gutes tue, lade ich mein Karma auf. Sie selbst hatte ihre Schwierigkeiten mit dem Loslassen. Zeit ihres Lebens verfolgte sie einen Traum: Ein kleines buddhistisches Kloster in Berlin bauen. Damals gab es noch kein Facebook und kein Crowdfunding. Dennoch gelang es ihr, eine große Crowd zu gewinnen, und bald hatte sie 10 000 Euro zusammen. Wie hat sie das geschafft? Ich habe viel von ihr gelernt. Im Grunde ist es ganz einfach: Achte darauf, dass Dein Leben zwischen Geben und Nehmen ausgewogen ist. Und Du wirst Glück finden. Achte auf Dein Karma.

Tausche Offenheit gegen Baupläne

Zwanzig Jahre später habe ich mir mit den Hartz-IV-Möbeln einen Namen gemacht. Die Baupläne verkaufe ich nicht. Ich verschenke sie. Na ja, das stimmt nicht ganz. Ich erwarte etwas zurück: eine Geschichte. Die Menschen bezahlen mit Offenheit. Geben und Nehmen. Mein

Karma. I can't buy myself an ice cream from this openness. But the compliments of so many people bring a smile to my face every time. Overwhelmed by the resonance: in the last two years, nearly ten thousand people have requested my plans. Many evenings, I receive up to eight hundred e-mails. Not only from Germany, but also from all over the world. What happened? Do people find my plans so amazing? DIY plans did already exist before my time. No, the truth is that in this project people see an alternative to the so highly praised market economy; to capitalism, which promised us all prosperity and has disappointed many. How can it be that so many companies have to cut jobs even when they are making record revenues? Why does a company actually constantly have to grow if it wants to remain competitive? At what point is a company full-grown? How has it happened that in countries such as Germany not enough families are being created and depression and burnout have become common complaints despite the high level of prosperity? Perhaps you have also asked these questions and fretted about your powerlessness.

The more I exchange ideas with the Crowd, the more I encounter like-minded people who think much the same as I do: people who have a desire for more warmth and equitableness, an economy that puts people's happiness at its center.

A New Era of Pioneers

All of a sudden, I started coming across movements that have such similar names: *Gemeinwohl Ökonomie* (2010, Common Good Economy) is the title of a book by the Austrian dancer (!) and cofounder of Attac, Christian Felber; "Gift Economy" is what the economist and former Harvard professor David C. Korten calls his philosophy; and "Informal Economy" is also such a catchword. "Collaborative Consumption," the philosophy of sharing that Rachel Botsman describes in a book, was even selected by *TIME Magazine* in 2011 as one of the most important ideas that will change the world.

Karma aufladen. Von dieser Offenheit kann ich mir kein Eis kaufen. Aber das Lob der vielen Menschen zaubert mir jedes Mal ein Lächeln ins Gesicht. Überwältigt von der Resonanz: In den letzten zwei Jahren haben fast zehntausend Menschen meine Pläne angefordert. An manchen Abenden bekomme ich bis zu achthundert E-Mails. Nicht nur aus Deutschland, sondern aus der ganzen Welt. Was ist passiert? Finden die Leute meine Pläne so toll? DIY-Pläne gab es doch schon vor meiner Zeit. Nein, die Wahrheit ist, die Menschen sehen in diesem Projekt eine Alternative zu der so hoch gepriesenen Marktwirtschaft. Der Kapitalismus, der uns allen Wohlstand versprach und viele enttäuschte. Wie kann es sein, dass manche Unternehmen Arbeitsplätze streichen müssen, auch wenn sie Rekordumsätze einfahren? Warum muss ein Unternehmen eigentlich ständig wachsen, wenn es konkurrenzfähig bleiben möchte? Ab wann ist ein Unternehmen ausgewachsen? Wie kommt es, dass in Ländern wie Deutschland trotz des hohen Wohlstands nicht genügend Familien entstehen und Depression und Burnout zu Volkskrankheiten werden? Vielleicht hast Du Dir diese Fragen auch gestellt und Dich über die Ohnmacht geärgert.

Je mehr ich mich mit der Crowd austausche, umso mehr stoße ich auf Gleichgesinnte, die so ähnlich denken wie ich. Menschen, die Sehnsucht nach mehr Wärme und Gerechtigkeit haben. Eine Wirtschaft, die wieder das Glück des Menschen in den Mittelpunkt stellt.

Eine neue Ära der Vordenker

Auf einmal stoße ich auf Bewegungen, die so ähnliche Namen tragen: *Gemeinwohl Ökonomie* (2010) heißt ein Buch von dem österreichischen Tänzer (!) und Attac-Mitgründer Christian Felber, »Gift Economy« betitelt der Ökonom und ehemalige Harvard-Professor David C. Korten seine Philosophie, »Informal Economy« ist auch so ein Stichwort. »Collaborative Consumption«, die Philosophie des Teilens, die Rachel Botsman in einem Buch beschreibt, wurde 2011 gar vom amerikanischen *TIME Magazine* zu einer der wichtigsten zehn Ideen gekürt, die die Welt verändern werden.

I don't know what year it will be when you read this here, but my clock shows 2012, and the last few years have been marked by crisis and upheaval: financial crisis, real-estate crisis, and the crisis in Greece. People are increasingly beginning to ask: What is actually happening with my money in the bank? What hourly wage does H&M pay the factory workers for one T-shirt? And the employees of the hardware store didn't know which forest the wood comes from either. Nonetheless, things have not remained at the question stage. People have looked for and found their answers. They are: do it yourself, co-working, car sharing, crowd funding, couch surfing, Wikipedia, open source, and Creative Commons. The key concept is: sharing.

Perhaps this, too, is only a hype that will once again pass, but I have the feeling that I am part of something really big here. And I would like to share my experiences with you.

What Exactly Is Karma Economy?

The idea behind Karma Economy is simple: you give more, you receive more. It changes how you look at supply and demand, the backbone of every market economy, on a larger scale. To keep it short: the foundations of economics teach us that what is ultimately concerned is the availability of resources, and since resources are often limited, the relationship between supply and demand is illustrated by the price. Since money does not play a very large role in our case, Karma Economy can produce a majority and thus equilibrium:

Maximization of Use

Goods can be distributed, exchanged, and used again and again by those who need them.

Optimization of Time

People can spend their free time in a way that is fun and brings them recognition while simultaneously helping others.

Ich weiß ja nicht, in welchem Jahr Du das hier liest, aber auf meiner Uhr steht 2012, die letzten Jahre waren geprägt von Krisen und Veränderungen: Finanzkrise, Immobilienkrise und Griechenlandkrise. Die Leute fangen vermehrt an zu fragen: Was passiert eigentlich mit meinem Geld in der Bank? Welchen Stundenlohn zahlt H&M den Fabrikarbeitern für ein T-Shirt? Und die Mitarbeiter im Baumarkt wussten auch nicht, aus welchem Wald das Holz kommt. Doch es ist nicht bei den Fragen geblieben. Die Menschen haben ihre Antworten gesucht und gefunden. Sie lauten: Do it yourself, Coworking, Carsharing, Crowdfunding, Couchsurfing, Wikipedia, Open Source und Creative Commons. Das Stichwort lautet: teilen.

Vielleicht ist das auch nur ein Hype, der wieder vorbei geht, doch ich habe das Gefühl, hier Teil von etwas ganz Großem zu sein. Und ich möchte gerne mit Euch meine Erfahrungen teilen.

Was genau ist Karma Economy?

Die Idee hinter Karma Economy ist simpel: Du gibst mehr, Du erhältst mehr. In einem größeren Maßstab ändert es die Sichtweise von Angebot und Nachfrage, dem Rückgrat jeder Marktwirtschaft. Um es kurz zu halten: Die Grundlagen der Wirtschaftswissenschaften lehren uns, dass es am Ende um die Bereitstellung von Ressourcen geht, und da die Ressourcen oft knapp sind, wird die Beziehung zwischen Angebot und Nachfrage durch den Preis abgebildet. Da in unserem Fall das Geld keine große Rolle spielt, kann Karma Economy ein Mehr erzeugen und somit ein Gleichgewicht herstellen:

Maximierung der Nutzung

Güter können verteilt, getauscht und immer wieder von denen, die sie benötigen, genutzt werden.

Optimierung der Zeit

Menschen können ihre Freizeit auf eine Weise verbringen, die ihnen Spaß und Anerkennung bringt, und gleichzeitig anderen helfen.

New Distribution of Resources

Both the goods and the time that people have at their disposal are distributed anew in order to make best use of them.

Efficiency in Solving Problems

In order to solve the problems of others, people spontaneously contribute what they have in their hands or head—and often do so right away.

The Karma Rule of Giving

Danny Iny, the author of *Engagement from Scratch!* (2011), was one of the first to write about Karma Economy. In a blog, he explained an important rule for not being exploited when giving. It is not about blindly offering your help to every person. "Help the helpful!" writes Iny. And be generous with your help. But to protect yourself, make sure that your help calls for a minimum of time and money. And: your help should bring the people you help maximum benefit. This distinguishes us Karma capitalists from firefighters, who sacrifice their time and lives almost unconditionally. Karma capitalists are not heroes!

Lots of People Achieve A Lot

Many people ask me how I manage to be so productive in such a short period of time (this book was created in four weeks—and I have a full-time job). This is naturally not possible without the input of the Crowd. But how does one build a community from scratch? The following pages will be of particular interest for people launching brands, creating new fans, or simply looking for friends.

The Yin-and-Yang Technique

This technique is influenced by Confucius and Bruce Lee.
It is clear that our lives are situated in a permanent field of tension between two poles: plus and minus, day and night, supply

Neuverteilung von Ressourcen

Sowohl die Güter als auch die Zeit, die Menschen zur Verfügung haben, werden neu verteilt, um das Beste aus ihnen zu machen.

Effizienz in der Problemlösung

Um die Probleme von anderen zu lösen, steuern Menschen spontan das bei, was sie in den Händen halten oder im Kopf haben – und dies oft augenblicklich.

Die Karma-Regel des Gebens

Danny Iny, Autor von *Engagement from Scratch!* (2011), ist einer der Ersten, die über Karma Economy schrieben. In einem Blog erklärt er eine wichtige Regel, um beim Geben nicht ausgebeutet zu werden. Es geht nicht darum, jedem Menschen blind Deine Hilfe anzubieten. »Hilf den Hilfsbereiten!«, schreibt Iny. Und sei großzügig mit Deiner Hilfe. Um Dich zu schützen, achte aber darauf, dass Deine Hilfe ein Minimum an Zeit und Geld beansprucht. Und: Deine Hilfe sollte dem Geholfenen ein Maximum an Nutzen bringen. Das unterscheidet uns Karma-Kapitalisten von der Feuerwehr, die nahezu bedingungslos ihre Zeit und ihr Leben opfern. Karma-Kapitalisten sind keine Helden!

Viele schaffen viel

Viele fragen mich, wie ich es schaffe, in so kurzer Zeit so produktiv zu sein (dieses Buch ist in vier Wochen entstanden – und ich habe einen Vollzeitjob). Klar geht das nicht ohne den Input der Crowd. Doch wie baut man aus dem Nichts eine Community auf? Die folgenden Seiten sind besonders für Menschen interessant, die unter Zeit- und Motivationsmangel leiden, und für Menschen, die Marken aufbauen, einen Fanstamm aufbauen oder einfach neue Freunde finden wollen. Lass es mich in einem Rap ausdrücken: »This is for people launching brands, creating new fans or simply looking for friends.«

and demand, giving and taking, and so forth. Followers of Confucius speak of yin and yang, marketing experts of push and pull. A company "pushes" a product on the market. In order to be able to increase the quality of the product, the company conducts a survey and "pulls" information from the market. These are two steps that usually occur separately. The push-and-pull strategy ultimately has the goal of selling more products. With pull, one creates demand.

For example, the Job Center in Germany (a cooperative relationship between the local welfare office and the employment agency) pushes money into households, and Hartz-IV welfare recipients attempt to pull as much money as possible from the government. The world thus consists of "push-and-pull types." Drivers of change are push types. Preservers of the status quo are pull types. What is your case? When are you a push type, and when a pull type?

The quite conscious use of yin-and-yang and/or push-and-pull techniques helps me to nearly double my time. How does this work? An allegory from martial arts helps us to understand:

Let's take a boxer and an aikido fighter.

What differentiates the two of them? Both have mastered techniques for attack and defense. One might also say: push and pull. The boxer raises his hands in order to prevent a punch in the face (pull) to then strike back with a counterpunch (push). These are two steps that follow quickly one after the other. In the case of the aikido fighter, this technique also exists. Only with one decisive difference: the aikido fighter has learned to perform attack and defense techniques in one step. In doing so, he uses the energy and weight of the attacker and redirects them into an attack. In the case of the aikido fighter, attack and defense are in fact only one step: push and pull in one movement. He saves time and energy! Everything that the boxer has to do in two arduous steps, the aikido fighter does in one. He gains time that he can then use lavishly for Japanese tea ceremonies. This has always fascinated

Die Yin-und-Yang-Technik

Diese Technik ist durch Konfuzius und Bruce Lee beeinflusst.

Es ist offensichtlich, dass unser Leben in einem ständigen Span-
nungsfeld zwischen zwei Polen befindet: Plus und Minus, Tag und
Nacht, Angebot und Nachfrage, Geben und Nehmen und so weiter.
Konfuzius-Anhänger sprechen von Yin und Yang. Marketingexperten
von Push und Pull. Eine Firma »pusht« ein Produkt in den Markt. Um
die Qualität des Produktes auswerten zu können, macht eine Firma
eine Befragung und zieht (Pull) sich Informationen aus dem Markt.
Das sind zwei Schritte, die in der Regel voneinander getrennt ablau-
fen. Die Push-und-Pull-Strategie hat am Ende das Ziel, mehr Produkte
zu verkaufen. Mit Pull erzeugt man eine Nachfrage.

Das Jobcenter »pusht« beispielsweise Geld in die Haushalte, und die
Hartz-IV-Empfänger versuchen, möglichst viel Geld aus dem Amt zu
ziehen (Pull). Die Welt besteht also aus »Push-und Pull-Typen«. Die
Veränderer sind Push-Typen. Die Status-quo-Bewahrer Pull-Typen.
Was ist mit Dir? Wann bist Du ein Push- und wann ein Pull-Typ?

Der sehr bewusste Einsatz von Yin-und-Yang- beziehungsweise Push-
und-Pull-Techniken hilft mir, meine Zeit fast zu verdoppeln. Wie das
geht? Ein Gleichnis aus dem Kampfsport bringt uns weiter:

Nehmen wir den Boxer und den Aikidokämpfer.

Was unterscheidet beide? Beide beherrschen Techniken für Angriff
und Abwehr. Man könnte auch sagen: Push und Pull.

Der Boxer nimmt die Hände hoch, um einen Schlag ins Gesicht zu
verhindern (Pull), um dann auszuholen zum Gegenschlag (Push). Das
sind zwei Schritte, die dicht aufeinanderfolgen. Beim Aikidokämpfer
gibt es diese Techniken auch. Nur mit einem entscheidenden Unterschied: Der Aikidokämpfer hat gelernt, Angriff- und Abwehrtechniken in
einem Schritt auszuführen. Dabei nutzt er die Energie und das Gewicht
des Angreifers und lenkt sie um in einen Angriff. Beim Aikidokämpfer
ist Angriff und Verteidigung also nur ein Schritt: Push und Pull in einer
Bewegung. Er spart Kraft und Zeit! Alles, was der Boxer in zwei müh-
samen Schritten machen muss, macht der Aikidokämpfer in einem.
Er gewinnt Zeit, die er dann ausgiebig für japanische Teezeremonien

me in the case of martial-arts fighters such as Bruce Lee. Although Bruce Lee is not a Japanese aikido fighter, nor does he drink tea, he was thin as a rake and nonetheless able to beat giants such as Chuck Norris. That's impressive!

Everyone Can Use the Yin-and-Yang Technique

Let's take the Hartz IV Möbel building plans. I send the building plans out into the world (push). In order to optimize my building plans, I have to ask experts for advice (pull) and, in order to measure the media resonance, even commission a press-cutting service to collect the clippings (pull). In order to motivate myself again, I have to hire a motivation coach (pull). These are four steps. In such a case, companies would commission four experts, pay budgets four times, and stipulate a time frame four times. I do all of this in one step. I differ in this respect from other open-source activists who simply offer their DIY plans for download without any controls. I quite deliberately do not do so.

And this is how it works: everyone who would like to have the building plan first has to answer some questions in an online form. In it, I ask what the motivation of the person ordering is (pull), in which newspaper they read about the building plan (pull), and oblige them to send me a story and photos (pull). There is also a free comment field (in which people generally commend me me) (pull). It's about giving and taking. And with only one on-line form (push), I have pulled four times. By means of this form, which incidentally the Australian Tammo Winkler from the Crowd programmed for me with Google Docs, an open-source software, I receive compliments every single day (pull). At this point, I would also like to give my heartfelt thanks to Tammo for the wonderful work (push; giving compliments is, by the way, also one of the push techniques). This motivates me! And that is much better than any remuneration in the world! People who do not want to participate do not receive the building plans. I don't want to give anything away and also don't want to have anything handed to

aufwenden kann. Das hat mich bei Martial-Arts-Kämpfern wie Bruce Lee immer fasziniert. Bruce Lee ist zwar kein japanischer Aikidokämpfer, trinkt auch keinen Tee, aber er war spindeldürr und konnte dennoch Riesen wir Chuck Norris besiegen. Das beeindruckt!

Jeder kann die Yin-und-Yang-Technik anwenden

Nehmen wir die Hartz-IV-Möbel-Baupläne. Ich sende die Baupläne in die Welt (Push). Um meine Baupläne zu optimieren, müsste ich Experten um Rat fragen (Pull), und um die Medienresonanz zu messen sogar einen Ausschnittdienst beauftragen, der Clippings zieht (Pull). Um mich immer wieder selbst zu motivieren, müsste ich einen Motivationscoach anstellen (Pull). Das sind vier Schritte. Firmen würden in diesem Fall vier Experten beauftragen, viermal Budgets bezahlen und viermal ein Zeitfenster aufsetzen. Ich mache das alles in einem Schritt. Ich unterscheide mich in dieser Hinsicht von anderen Open-Source-Aktivisten, die einfach ihre DIY-Pläne unkontrolliert zum Download anbieten. Das mache ich ganz bewusst nicht.

Und so geht's: Jeder, der den Bauplan haben möchte, muss erstmal einige Fragen in einem Onlineformular beantworten. Hier frage ich ab, worin die Motivation der Besteller besteht (Pull), in welcher Zeitschrift sie davon gelesen haben (Pull) und verpflichte sie, dass sie mir eine Geschichte und Fotos schicken (Pull). Es gibt noch ein freies Kommentarfeld (wo mir die Leute meist ihr Lob aussprechen, Pull). Es geht um Geben und Nehmen. Und mit nur einem Onlineformular (Push) habe ich viermal »gepullt«. Durch dieses Formular, welches mir übrigens der Australier Tammo Winkler aus der Crowd mit Google Docs, einer Open-Source-Software, programmiert hat, bekomme ich tagtäglich Komplimente (Pull). An dieser Stelle ein großes Dankeschön an Tammo für die grandiose Arbeit (Push; Komplimente machen zählt übrigens auch zu den Push-Techniken). Das motiviert mich! Und das ist viel besser als jedes Gehalt der Welt! Wer nicht mitmachen möchte, bekommt die Baupläne nicht. Ich möchte nichts verschenken und auch nichts geschenkt bekommen. Das unterscheidet mich von einem Gutmenschen und einem Bittsteller. Ich bin Karma-Kapitalist.

me. That differentiates me from a do-gooder or a supplicant. I am a Karma capitalist.

Yin and Yang in Everyday Working Life

Here is another example: in everyday working life, working hours and education training are two fundamentally separate states. One either goes to work (push) or one goes to education training (pull). Most people also separate work (push) from relaxation (pull). I admit that in many cases work is also simply only work. But let's attempt to apply the yin-and-yang technique here. It's sometimes the subtle details that make the difference.

For instance, I go to meetings with customers or presentations at which I am expected to provide content for people's benefit (push) with basically the following attitude. I do not think: how can I "push" my content onto my listeners most impressively, but I instead think: what are the three things that I can now learn from the customers or the audience (pull)? I have learned so much from my customers and the Crowd. For example, a customer brought me to the website www.ted.com. And it cost me neither time nor money. I receive a fee (pull) for my presentations and workshops, and I get education training for free at the same time. And all of this in one step without any extra effort. Cool, don't you think?

Try it out. What is push in your life, what is pull? How can you link the two of them so that you can do them in one step? This saves time. That is why I often need half as much time for the same things as other people. If an example springs to your mind, then be sure to write it on my pinboard at www.facebook.com/hartziv moebel (oops, a pull technique already crept in here again . . .)

How did I actually build up the Crowd and manage to get hundreds of volunteers to work for free on a project like this book?

Ladies and Gentleman, it's time to reveal the secret. Here is my recipe for success, a manifesto for making work easier for people who have a great interest in designing their social environment. I call it:

Yin und Yang im Berufsalltag

Hier ein anderes Beispiel: Im Berufsleben sind Arbeitszeit und Weiterbildung zwei grundsätzlich getrennte Zustände. Entweder man geht
zur Arbeit (Push) oder man geht zur Weiterbildung (Pull). Die meisten
Menschen trennen auch Arbeit (Push) von Erholung (Pull). Ich gebe
zu, in vielen Fällen ist die Arbeit auch einfach nur Arbeit. Doch versuchen wir mal, hier die Yin-und-Yang-Technik einzusetzen. Manchmal
sind es subtile Details, die den Unterschied ausmachen.

Beispielsweise gehe ich an Kundentermine oder Vorträge, wo von mir
erwartet wird, einen Inhalt zum Besten zu geben (Push), grundsätzlich
mit folgender Einstellung ran. Ich denke nicht: Wie kann ich am ein-
drücklichsten meinen Content in meine Zuhörerschaft »pushen«, sondern ich denke: Was sind die drei Dinge, die ich jetzt von den Kunden
oder vom Publikum lernen kann (Pull)? Ich habe so viel von Kunden
und der Crowd gelernt. Auf die Webseite www.ted.com hat mich zum
Beispiel ein Kunde gebracht. Und es hat mich weder extra Zeit noch
Geld gekostet. Ich bekomme ein Honorar (Pull) für meine Vorträge und
Workshops und dann noch eine Weiterbildung gratis dazu. Und das
alles in einem Schritt ohne Extraaufwand. Cool, oder?

Probiere es aus. Was in Deinem Leben ist Push, was ist Pull? Und wie
kann man beides so verknüpfen, dass Du es in einem Schritt ausfüh-
ren kannst? Das spart Zeit. Ich brauche deshalb oftmals halb so viel
Zeit für die gleichen Dinge wie andere. Wenn Dir ein Beispiel einfällt,
dann schreibe es unbedingt auf meine Pinnwand auf www.facebook.
com/hartzivmoebel (ups, schon wieder hat sich hier eine Pull-Technik
eingeschlichen ...).

Wie habe ich eigentlich die Crowd aufgebaut und Hunderte von Frei-
willigen gewinnen können, die unentgeltlich an einem Projekt wie diesem Buch arbeiten?

Ladies and Gentleman, es wird Zeit, das Geheimnis zu lüften. Hier
mein Erfolgsrezept. Ein Manifest, um die Arbeit für Menschen, die ein
großes Interesse haben ihr soziales Umfeld zu gestalten, einfacher zu
machen. Ich nenne es:

The Karma Sutra in 7 Steps (or: Social Design Manifesto)

Please do not confuse this with the *Kama Sutra*.
According to Hindu tradition, a Sutra is a teaching in verse form, a type of guide in rhymes. Here comes my Sutra for the Karma Economy in seven steps, which may bring you the gift of a large crowd and lots of Karma:

1. Base: Explain the foundation for your actions

Do you have a great idea, a wonderful product, or a fantastic service—in short, something great—to offer? Super, other people probably do, too. Explain what the foundation—the base—of what you have to offer is. What I have to offer are DIY building plans. That's great but there is something else behind it. An attitude: build more, buy less—this is my base. Formulate a base that is larger than what you have to offer and you will obtain a crowd!

2. Chase: Tell your story and let us be a part of your quest

Chase is a quest, a passionate search, a goal. I invented the first Hartz-IV-Möbel in order to impress my fiancée. That is my story, my chase. What it's ultimately about for me is love. Scriptwriters call such a thing plot and would film my chase as "boy meets girl." What is behind what you have to offer? What exactly do you want to change in the world? How would your film go? The more personal and simple your idea is, the more your crowd will be able to identify with it. Tell them your story. What is your chase?

Das Karma-Sutra der 7 Schritte (oder Social Design Manifesto)

Bitte nicht mit dem *Kamasutra* verwechseln.

Ein Sutra ist nach hinduistischer Tradition eine Lehre in Versform, eine Art Ratgeber in Reimen. Hier kommt mein Sutra für die Karma Economy in 7 Schritten, die Dir eine große Crowd und viel Karma bescheren möge:

1. Base: Erkläre das Fundament Deines Handelns

Du hast eine tolle Idee, ein tolles Produkt oder einen tollen Service, kurz: ein tolles Angebot? Super, das haben andere wahrscheinlich auch. Mach deutlich, auf welchem Fundament, auf welcher Basis Dein Angebot beruht. Mein Angebot sind DIY-Baupläne. Das ist schön, doch da steckt noch etwas Größeres dahinter. Eine Haltung: konstruieren statt konsumieren (build more, buy less) – das ist meine Base. Formuliere eine Base, die größer als Dein Angebot ist, und Du wirst eine Crowd gewinnen!

2. Chase: Erzähle Deine Geschichte und lass uns an Deiner Suche teilhaben

Chase ist eine Jagd, eine leidenschaftliche Suche, ein Ziel. Ich habe das erste Hartz-IV-Möbel erfunden, um meine Verlobte zu beeindrucken. Das ist meine Story, mein Chase. Es geht bei mir letztendlich um die Liebe. Drehbuchautoren nennen so etwas Plot und würden meinen Chase als »Boy-meets-Girl«-Geschichte verfilmen. Was steckt hinter Deinem Angebot? Was genau willst Du verändern auf der Welt? Wie würde Dein Film aussehen? Je persönlicher und einfacher, umso mehr kann sich Deine Crowd mit Deiner Idee identifizieren. Erzähle ihnen Deine Geschichte. Was ist Dein Chase?

3. Face: Give your idea a face, a name, or a symbol

Give what you have to offer a name, a team, or a face. If you are shy, invent a little animal or a symbol. For the crowd, it is important to see who stands behind the idea. Who is responsible? This is the reason why large, successful (faceless) corporations again and again work with faces. At IKEA, next to a lamp stands a portrait of its designer. At Kentucky Fried Chicken, a nice grandfather smiles at us. At the entrance to big supermarkets there is an overview of the team with photos and names. Try it out. Give what you have to offer an engaging face!

4. Place: Give us a location where everything comes together

A crowd needs a central location. It can be an Internet page or a Facebook fan page. Naturally, a real location is the best: a camp, a café, a central office. For the writing of this book, I got involved in the betahaus co-working office in Berlin. That was the place for the production of the book. You don't have to build an entire world like BMW (the BMW Welt, an experience and delivery center of the BMW brand) or a land like Disney (Disneyland). It is sometimes sufficient to connect your idea with a city that opens up entire worlds in the heads of the crowd. That's why there is the Berliner Hocker (stool) and the Neukoelln Desk. Give your crowd a place!

5. Space: Be generous with free space and encounter criticism with courage

Crowds are not fans that blindly follow you like a rock star. They are followers. They follow you as long as you respect their needs. Be courageous and generous. Allow your crowd free space in which they are able to express themselves and are allowed to criticize you. They will thank you for it with recognition, word-of-mouth recommendations, and also financial support! That's why I believe in Creative Commons and do not censor any criticism on

3. Face: Gib Deiner Idee ein Gesicht, einen Namen oder ein Symbol

Gib Deinem Angebot einen Namen, ein Team oder ein Gesicht. Wenn Du schüchtern bist, erfinde ein Tierchen oder ein Symbol. Für die Crowd ist es wichtig zu sehen, wer dahinter steckt. Wer trägt die Verantwortung? Das ist der Grund, warum große erfolgreiche (gesichtslose) Konzerne immer wieder mit Gesichtern arbeiten. Bei IKEA hängt neben der Lampe ein Porträt ihres Designers. Bei Kentucky Fried Chicken lächelt uns ein netter Opa entgegen, bei Saturn gibt es am Eingang eine Teamübersicht mit Fotos und Namen. Probiere es aus. Gib Deinem Angebot ein verbindliches Gesicht!

4. Place: Stelle uns einen Ort zur Verfügung, wo alles zusammenkommt

Eine Crowd braucht einen zentralen Ort. Das kann eine Internetseite oder eine Facebook-Fanpage sein. Am besten ist natürlich ein echter Ort. Ein Camp, ein Café, eine Zentrale. Ich habe mich für das Schreiben dieses Buches in dem Berliner Coworking-Büro betahaus eingeschlossen. Das war der Place für die Buchproduktion. Du musst nicht gleich wie BMW eine ganze Welt (die BMW Welt) bauen oder wie Disney ein Land (das Disneyland). Manchmal genügt es, Deine Idee mit einer Stadt in Verbindung zu setzen, die in der Crowd ganze Welten im Kopf aufmacht. Deshalb gibt es den Berliner Hocker und den Neukoelln Desk. Gib Deiner Crowd einen Platz!

5. Space: Sei großzügig mit Freiräumen und mutig für Kritik

Crowds sind keine Fans, die Dir blind folgen wie einem Rockstar. Sie sind Follower. Sie folgen Dir, solange Du ihre Bedürfnisse verteidigst. Sei mutig und großzügig, gewähre Deiner Crowd Freiräume, in denen sie sich ausdrücken kann und Dich kritisieren darf. Sie dankt es Dir mit Anerkennung, Mundpropaganda und auch finanzieller Unterstützung! Deshalb setze ich auf Creative Commons und zensiere keine Kritiken bei Facebook. Auch in diesem Buch gebe ich der Crowd viel Raum.

Facebook. I also give the Crowd lots of space in this book. Be courageous: ask for and accept criticism! Allocate applause equitably. Be generous and give your crowd space.

6. Trace: Show your traces and make your path transparent

Trace means the marks that you leave behind. Do not cover them up! Every one of us makes mistakes. Stand by them and take responsibility. If money flows or decisions need to be made, make it transparent. This is why I have disclosed where the money from the crowd funding campaign for this book is going: printing and wood. And if there is anything left over, I will finance my wedding with it. Do not be ashamed of the personal needs that you are attempting to resolve with the help of the crowd, but instead stand by them. The distinguished expert on advertising, Wally Olins, wrote on his Internet page that he has a weakness for fast cars. The crowd will love you and forgive you if you remain honest and show your path, your marks—your traces.

7. Days: Be unlimited in your heart but keep limits on time and energy

Days means: count your days! Specify the end before you begin! This prevents delusions of grandeur and frustration. Everything in the world is limited. The designer Stefan Sagmeister closes his office every seven years in order to take time off. This is also a form of limitedness. That's the reason why I enjoy playing with numbers so much: building the Berliner Hocker in 10 minutes, the 24-Euro-Chair in 24 hours. That's why I invented the One-Hour-Power Team, in which everyone has been able to be involved in this book with a time commitment of a maximum of 60 minutes. I love crowd-funding pages and eBay because of the countdown. Do not make things infinite but instead finite.

Sei mutig, fordere und ertrage Kritik! Verteile den Applaus gerecht. Sei großzügig und gib ihnen Space.

6. Trace: Lege Deine Spuren offen und mache Deinen Weg transparent

Trace meint Spuren, die Du hinterlässt. Verwische sie nicht! Jeder von uns macht Fehler. Stehe zu ihnen, und nimm die Verantwortung an. Wenn Geld fließt oder Entscheidungen zu treffen sind, mach es transparent. Deshalb habe ich offen gelegt, wohin das Geld aus der Crowdfunding-Kampagne für dieses Buch geht: Druck und Holz. Und wenn etwas überbleibt, finanziere ich meine Hochzeitsfeier damit. Schäm Dich nicht für Deine Bedürfnisse, die Du mithilfe der Crowd zu lösen versuchst, sondern stehe dazu. Werbekoryphäe Wally Olins schrieb auf seiner Internetseite, dass er ein Faible für schnelle Autos hat. Die Crowd wird Dich lieben und Dir verzeihen, wenn Du ehrlich bleibst und sie offen legst: Deinen Weg, Deine Spuren – Deine Traces.

7. Days: Sei unendlich im Herzen, aber endlich mit Zeit und Kraft

Days meint: Zähle die Tage! Lege das Ende fest, bevor Du anfängst! Es verhindert Größenwahn und Frust. Alles auf der Welt ist endlich. Der Designer Stefan Sagmeister schließt alle sieben Jahre sein Büro, um sich eine Auszeit zu nehmen. Das ist auch eine Form von Endlichkeit. Das ist der Grund, warum ich so gerne mit Zahlen spiele: Den Berliner Hocker in 10 Minuten bauen. Den 24-Euro-Chair in 24 Stunden. Deswegen habe ich das One-Hour-Power Team erfunden, wo jeder mit einem zeitlichen Einsatz von maximal 60 Minuten bereits an diesem Buch mitwirken konnte. Ich liebe Crowdfunding-Seiten oder eBay wegen des Countdowns. Mach es nicht endlos, sondern endlich.

Everyone Can Build a Crowd!

The fact that institutes, celebrities, scientists, and activists find followers is obvious. But can everyone actually do so? Even the fast-food restaurant around the corner? Yes! Are you familiar with Mustafa's Gemüsekebap in Berlin-Kreuzberg? 10,000 Facebook fans! Okay, he simply has the most delicious vegetable kebabs in the city. Let me be extreme for a moment: How about a location that we prefer to avoid, of which we are even afraid, let's say, a dental practice? Can a dentist build a crowd? Well, then take a look at the practice of Dr. Irena Vaksman in San Francisco. She has over 6,000 Facebook fans. And that is not because she is famous or has a particular specialization. No, she uses the seven steps of the Karma Sutra. Look at her videos on Facebook, where she (face) says directly that the need for information (base) is behind her expertise as a dentist. She uses her Facebook pinboard (place) as a service platform for responding to the needs and questions (space) of the crowd. Criticism is openly discussed on the pinboard (trace). On her pinboard, she explains that what ultimately concerns her is leading a happy life with two small children and her husband (chase). So that she does not become a workaholic, she limits her working time with the help of open-source tools such as Google Calendar or a task manager on her iPhone (days).

My crowd has drawn up a list of best-practice examples that can teach you a great deal. Are you interested? Then request the best-practice list now. The price: zero euros. But we expect you to add a good example to the list so that it grows. More information is available here: www.hartzivmoebel.com

An Unfulfilled Dream

I learned all of this from the crowd and, above all, from the woman who searched for and found her own crowd as a "bright mother" (face). Her foundation was the belief in enlightenment (base), and what drove her was the search for fulfillment out of grief (chase).

Jeder kann eine Crowd aufbauen!

Dass Institute, Promis, Wissenschaftler und Aktivisten eine Anhänger-
schaft finden, leuchtet ein. Doch kann das wirklich jeder? Auch der
Imbiss um die Ecke? Ja! Kennst Du Mustafas Gemüsekebap in Berlin-
Kreuzberg? 10 000 Facebook-Fans! Okay, der hat einfach den leckers-
ten Gemüsekebap der Stadt. Lass mich mal ganz extrem werden: Wie
wäre es mit einem Ort, den wir eher meiden, vor dem wir gar Angst haben:
Eine Zahnarztpraxis beispielsweise. Kann ein Zahnarzt eine Crowd aufbauen? Na, dann schau Dir die Praxis von Dr. Irena Vaksman in San
Francisco an. Sie hat über 6 000 Facebook-Fans. Und das nicht, weil
sie bekannt ist oder eine besondere Spezialisierung hat. Nein, sie
wendet die 7 Schritte des Karma-Sutra an. Schau Dir ihre Videos bei
Facebook an, wo sie (Face) geradeaus sagt, dass hinter ihrer Expertise als Zahnärztin das Bedürfnis nach Aufklärung (Base) steht. Sie
nutzt ihre Facebook-Pinnwand (Place) als Serviceplattform, um die
Bedürfnisse und Fragen (Space) der Crowd zu beantworten. Kritik
wird auf der Pinnwand offen besprochen (Trace). Hier erklärt sie, dass
es ihr letztendlich darum geht, ein glückliches Leben mit zwei kleinen Kindern und ihrem Ehemann zu führen (Chase). Um nicht zum
Workaholic zu werden, begrenzt sie ihre Arbeitszeit mithilfe von Open-
Source-Tools wie Google Calendar oder einem Task Manager auf dem
iPhone (Days).

Meine Crowd hat eine Liste mit Best-Practice-Beispielen erstellt, von
denen man viel lernen kann. Bist Du daran interessiert? Dann fordere
die Best-Practice-Liste jetzt an. Der Preis: Null Euro. Aber wir erwar-
ten, dass Du die Liste um ein gutes Beispiel ergänzt, damit sie wächst.
Hier gibt's mehr Infos: www.hartzivmoebel.com

Ein unerfüllter Traum

Das alles habe ich von der Crowd gelernt und vor allem von der Frau,
die als »lichte Mutter« (Face) ihre eigene Crowd gesucht und gefunden hatte. Ihr Fundament war der Glaube an Erleuchtung (Base), ihr
Antrieb war die Suche nach Erfüllung aus der Trauer (Chase). Sie

She wanted to build a temple for like-minded individuals (place) in order to create space for meditation and calm (space). In the process, she communicated openly about how much donation money had already been collected (trace). Until the very end, Co Hanh Nhu lived for this dream, which never came true. She died unexpectedly of a stroke at the age of forty-two.

If I have learned anything from this story, then this: Do you have a dream? Fight for it. Seek out like-minded individuals. Do not hesitate. Whether it works out or not: take care of your Karma. Since one thing is now already clear: our days in this beautiful world are numbered.

wollte für Gleichgesinnte einen Tempel bauen (Place), um Raum für Meditation und Ruhe (Space) zu schaffen. Dabei kommunizierte sie offen, wie viel Spendengeld schon gesammelt wurde (Trace). Co Hanh Nhu lebte bis zuletzt für diesen Traum, der niemals wahr wurde. Sie starb unerwartet an einem Schlaganfall, im Alter von 42 Jahren.

Wenn ich etwas aus dieser Geschichte gelernt habe, dann das: Hast Du einen Traum? Kämpfe für ihn, suche Gleichgesinnte. Zögere nicht. Ob es klappt oder nicht: Achte auf Dein Karma. Denn eines ist jetzt schon klar: Unsere Tage auf dieser schönen Welt sind gezählt.

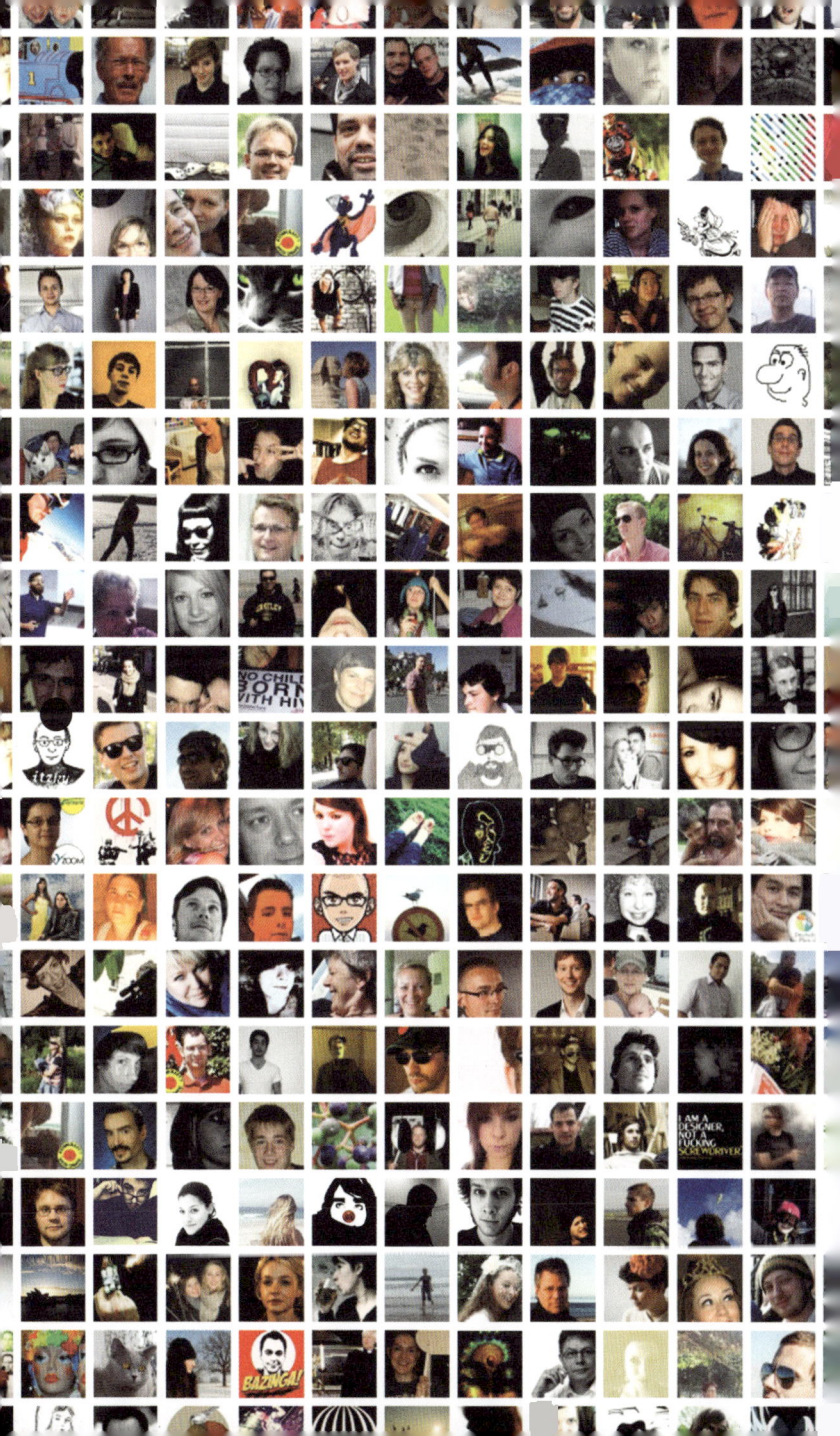

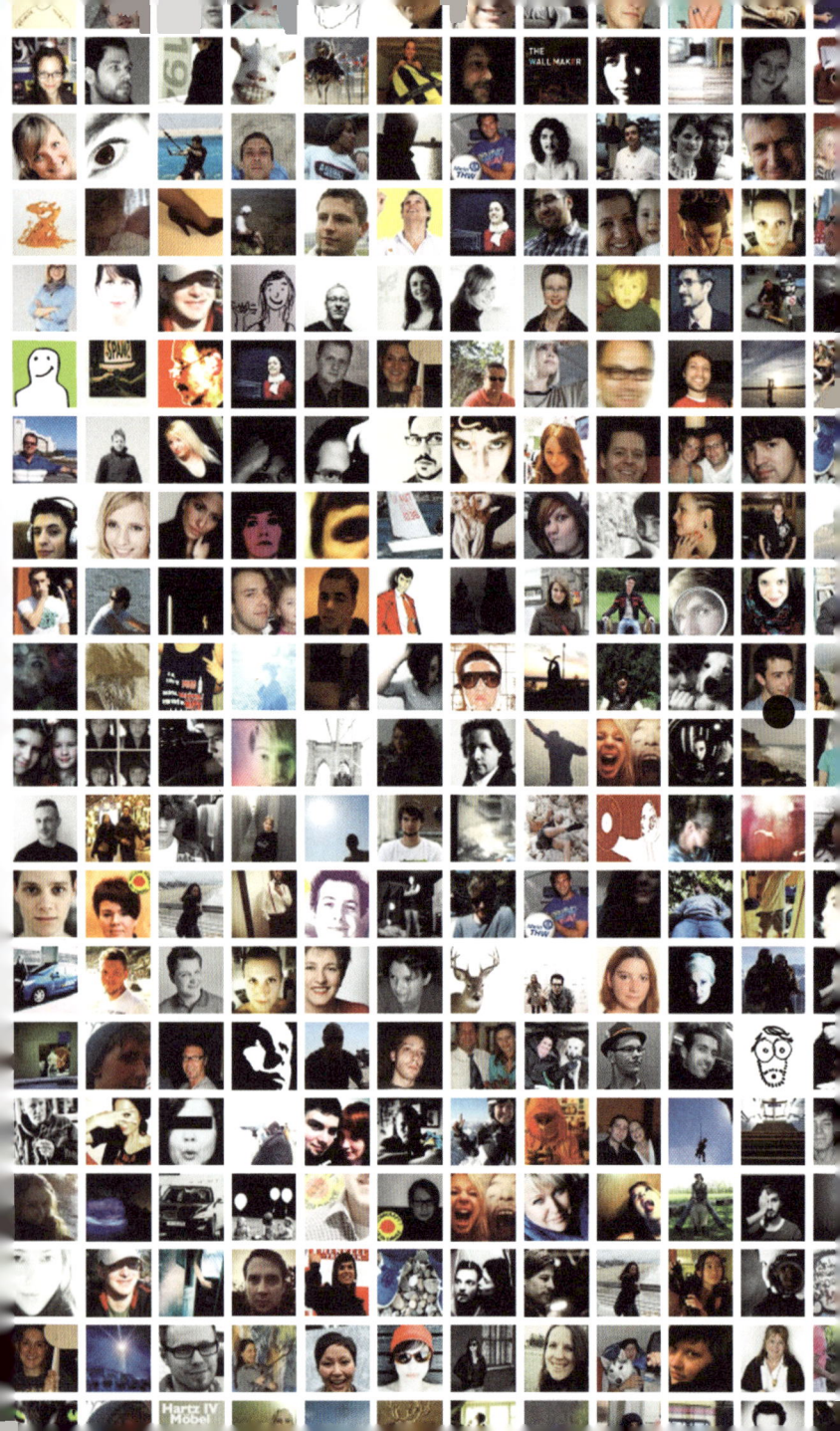

Thank You / **Danke**

I dedicate this book to the Crowd, my wife Luise, and the bright mother / Dieses Buch widme ich der Crowd, meiner Frau Luise und der lichten Mutter.

Yours / Euer Van Bo

Many thanks to / Vielen Dank an:
Corinne Rose, dan pearlman GmbH, Tom Hansing (www.offenewerkstaetten.org), Charlotte Klingspor & VHS City West, Jan-Phillip Holzenburg, Arash Serkani, Daniela Kleint

This book would not have been possible without the Crowd: thanks go to Supa-Dupa Team, One-Hour-Power Team, and the 500 most active people in my Facebook Crowd for the caring and sharing / Dieses Buch wäre nicht möglich ohne die Crowd: Dank geht an das Supa-Dupa Team, One-Hour-Power Team und die 500 aktivsten Menschen meiner Facebook-Crowd für die Zuwendung und das Teilen

Supa-Dupa Team:
Kay Strasser, Kristin Hensel, Birgit S. Bauer, Tran Kinh Manh, Stefanie Greuel, Inga Dehl, Sebastian Sieber, Regine Lin, Ulrike Stier, Simon Frambach, Sebastian Körtels, Sandra Schauer, Bruno Miguel Fernandes Maltez, Fine Heininger, Hoang Hoa Nguyen, Alexandra Kahl, Carolina López Tomás, Tammo Winkler, Sabine Schmidt, Nele Ouwens, Alessa Joosten, Jesko Bendmann, Jessica Hanke, Katrin Ehm, Bela Lehrnickel, Making-of-Filmteam (Nina Hautumm, Anja Bleyl, Svea Vogel), formulor.de

One-Hour-Power Team:
Sandra Ae-Sim Schleicher, Susanne Papawassiliu, Andrea Kamphuis, Sonja Königsberg, Hans Pul, Simon Wind, Mathias Wetzl, Julia Meyer, Christoph Janitzek, Julia Baier, Olga Reimgen,

Stanislav Bugaev, Saskia Vinueza, Phil-Gordan Zameit, Yasmin Malika von Nagy, Ulrich Große, Christian Weichel, Juri Itin

Thanks for the contributions / Danke für die Spenden:
This book was co-financed via www.startnext.de through a Crowd-funding campaign. Thanks are extended to the 334 startnext supporters who believed in this book from the very outset – with special thanks to / Dieses Buch wurde kofinanziert via www.startnext.de durch eine Crowdfunding-Kampagne. Danke an die 334 Startnext-Supporter, die von Anfang an an dieses Buch geglaubt haben, insbesondere:
Jana Lübeck, David Katzenstein, Marcel Neumann, Myriam Sonanini, Michael Hofer, Sandra Schauer, Andreas Kücker, Karin Henz, Isger Janson, Patrick Jedamzik, Martin Flaischerowitz, Ulrike R. Schulze, Marfos Marktforschung GmbH, Icon Added Value GmbH, Birgit S. Bauer, Marie Voigt, Nina Hautumm & Hendrik von Beust, Marco Kerber, Nicole »Joshi« Benthin & Jork A. Dieter (dan pearlman), Jens Heinemann, Clara Suarez, Cristina Steingräber, Eliane Schilliger, Hendrik Beckmann, Walter Herrmann, Markus Ziegler, Marcus Schulz, Heinz & Theresia Kaiser, Manfred Stoffl, Max Schultes, Tobias Krullmann, Gabriele Kern, Emal Ghamsharick, Sonja Königsberg, Paul Führing, Karen Pasig, Joachim Simon, Daria A. Domogala, Patrick Völkl, Maike Haza, Sascha Stoltenow, Gerald Neu, Christoph Potthof, Michael Staatz, Uwe Linke, Uwe Küllmar, Michael Schmidt, Lisa Leukel, Duncan McFartley, Andrea Kamphuis, M. Brückner, Frederic Matthiss, Denis Bartelt, Stefanie Stich, Lisa Buchauer, Sven Herold

Thanks for the Karma Cooperation / Danke für die Karma-Kooperation:
Museum für Kommunikation Frankfurt und Berlin, Modulor, Kulturverein Schloss Goldegg, Berner Fachhochschule, *NEON*, betahaus & Open Design City, IDZ Berlin, Goethe-Institut Montreal

Editor / Herausgeber: **Van Bo Le-Mentzel**

Editing / Redaktion: **Van Bo Le-Mentzel, Rebecca Sandbichler, Marie Voigt, Emrullah Gümüşsoy, Steffen Schumann, Axel Watzke**

Image editing / Bildredaktion **Community chapter:**
Emrullah Gümüşsoy

Copyediting / Verlagslektorat: **Dawn Michelle d'Atri, Birte Kreft**

Translations / Übersetzungen: **Amy J. Klement**

Art direction / Artdirection: **anschlaege.de**

Graphic design / Grafikdesign: **Frederike Wagner, Design Bureau kokliko**

Typeface / Schrift: **Arial**

Reproductions / Reproduktionen: **Jan Scheffler, prints professional**

Production / Verlagsherstellung: **Katja Jaeger**

Paper / Papier: **Tauro Offset, 120 g/m²**

Printing and binding / Gesamtherstellung: **DZA Druckerei zu Altenburg GmbH, Altenburg**

Published by / Erschienen im
Hatje Cantz Verlag
Zeppelinstrasse 32
73760 Ostfildern
Germany / Deutschland
Tel. +49 711 4405-200
Fax +49 711 4405-220
www.hatjecantz.com

Hatje Cantz books are available internationally at selected bookstores.
For more information about our distribution partners, please visit our homepage at
www.hatjecantz.com

ISBN 978-3-7757-3395-3
Printed in Germany

Photo credits / Fotonachweis:
Inner cover, front / Umschlaginnenseite, vorne: **Cem Guenes**, pp. / S. 6–7: **Daniela Kleint**; 18: **Kay Strasser**; 19: **Emrullah Gümüşsoy**;
74–77: **Emrullah Gümüşsoy**; 78–79: **Nadine Krüger**; 80: private / privat **(Geert Vullings)**; 81 left / links: private / privat **(Pieter van der Kooij)**; 81 right / rechts: **Michaela Siegl**; 82: private / privat **(Matthias just4fun.)**; 83: private / privat **(Konrad Jünger)**; 84–85: **Janina Schuster (j.schuster@hbk-bs.de)**; 86–95: **Emrullah Gümüşsoy**; 96 left / links: private / privat **(Jesko Bendmann)**; 96 top right and bottom / rechts oben und unten: private / privat **(Georg W.)**; 97: **Robert J. Swartz**; 98: **Judith Langner**; 99: **Linnéa Weitkamp**; 100: **Hartmut Raiser**; 101: private / privat **(Laura Ameskamp)**; 102: **Osman Erdogan (www.fd-m.de)**; 103: private / privat **(Dusan R.)**; 104: **Ib Voss Pedersen**; 105: **Katrin Brunner**; 106: private / privat **(Andreas Doerig)**; 107: **Vittorio Zincone**; 108: **Robert Ziegler, Stefanie Ammon ® £0 12 VG Bild Kunst, Bonn**; 109: **Jan Vailhé**; 110: **Peter Empl**; 111: private / privat **(Steven)**; inner cover, back / Umschlaginnenseite, hinten: **Van Bo Le-Mentzel**

Portraitcollage / Porträtcollage, pp. / S. 140–41: **Stefanie Greuel**
Karmulor motif for the postcard / Karmulor-Motiv für die Postkarte: **Jork A. Dieter**
Cover illustration / Umschlagabbildung: **Van Bo Le-Mentzel & anschlaege.de**

All illustrations (unless otherwise specified) by / Alle Illustrationen (sofern nicht anders angegeben) von **Van Bo Le-Mentzel**

Traffic blue / Verkehrsblau –
approx. / etwa RAL 5017

Perfect for the Kreuzberg-36-Chair and kitchen walls /
Perfekt für den Kreuzberg-36-Chair und Küchenwände

hartz IV moebel.com